CAMBRIDGE LIBRARY COLLECTION

Books of enduring scholarly value

Women's Writing

The later twentieth century saw a huge wave of academic interest in women's writing, which led to the rediscovery of neglected works from a wide range of genres, periods and languages. Many books that were immensely popular and influential in their own day are now studied again, both for their own sake and for what they reveal about the social, political and cultural conditions of their time. A pioneering resource in this area is Orlando: Women's Writing in the British Isles from the Beginnings to the Present (http://orlando.cambridge.org), which provides entries on authors' lives and writing careers, contextual material, timelines, sets of internal links, and bibliographies. Its editors have made a major contribution to the selection of the works reissued in this series within the Cambridge Library Collection, which focuses on non-fiction publications by women on a wide range of subjects from astronomy to biography, music to political economy, and education to prison reform.

Social Studies

Lady Jane Francesca Wilde (1821–96) is today best known as the mother of Oscar Wilde (1854–1900), but in her lifetime was famous in her own right as a fervent supporter of Irish Nationalism, writing Nationalist poems under the pseudonym of *Speranza* (Hope). After the death of her husband in 1876, Lady Wilde wrote to support herself, her other works including essays, literary criticism and travel writing. She was also a strong supporter of feminism and the campaign for female suffrage and legal rights. This volume, first published in 1893, contains a collection of essays on various topics of importance to Lady Wilde, including feminism, good manners and aesthetic clothing, with short biographies of Irish Nationalist leaders. This volume was Lady Wilde's last published work, and provides a valuable example of her writing style and the influence of the aesthetic movement on social behaviour. For more information on this author, see http://orlando. cambridge.org/public/svPeople?person_id=wildja

G000061407

Cambridge University Press has long been a pioneer in the reissuing of out-of-print titles from its own backlist, producing digital reprints of books that are still sought after by scholars and students but could not be reprinted economically using traditional technology. The Cambridge Library Collection extends this activity to a wider range of books which are still of importance to researchers and professionals, either for the source material they contain, or as landmarks in the history of their academic discipline.

Drawing from the world-renowned collections in the Cambridge University Library, and guided by the advice of experts in each subject area, Cambridge University Press is using state-of-the-art scanning machines in its own Printing House to capture the content of each book selected for inclusion. The files are processed to give a consistently clear, crisp image, and the books finished to the high quality standard for which the Press is recognised around the world. The latest print-on-demand technology ensures that the books will remain available indefinitely, and that orders for single or multiple copies can quickly be supplied.

The Cambridge Library Collection will bring back to life books of enduring scholarly value (including out-of-copyright works originally issued by other publishers) across a wide range of disciplines in the humanities and social sciences and in science and technology.

Social Studies

Jane Francesca Wilde

CAMBRIDGE
UNIVERSITY PRESS

CAMBRIDGE UNIVERSITY PRESS

Cambridge, New York, Melbourne, Madrid, Cape Town, Singapore,
São Paolo, Delhi, Dubai, Tokyo, Mexico City

Published in the United States of America by Cambridge University Press, New York

www.cambridge.org
Information on this title: www.cambridge.org/9781108021951

© in this compilation Cambridge University Press 2010

This edition first published 1893
This digitally printed version 2010

ISBN 978-1-108-02195-1 Paperback

SOCIAL STUDIES

BY

LADY WILDE

AUTHOR OF

'NOTES ON MEN, WOMEN AND BOOKS,' ETC.

WARD & DOWNEY

12 YORK STREET COVENT GARDEN LONDON

1893

(All Rights reserved).

CONTENTS.

—o—

WORKS BY LADY WILDE.

Ancient Irish Legends.   Crown 8vo, 6s.

Ancient Irish Cures and Charms.   Crown 8vo, 6s.

Driftwood from Scandinavia.

Notes on Men, Women and Books.   Crown 8vo, 6s.

Eritis Sicut Deus.   3 vols.
(From the German.)

Sidonia the Sorceress.
(From the German.)

The Glacier Land.   (Dumas.)

The Wanderer and his Home.   (Lamartine.)

Pictures from the First French Revolution.

The Future Life.   (Swedenborg.)

Poems, Original, and Translated from the French, Spanish, Portuguese, Italian, German, Swedish, and Danish Languages.

SOCIAL STUDIES.

———o———

THE BONDAGE OF WOMAN.

FOR six thousand years the history of woman has been a mournful record of helpless resignation to social prejudice and legal tyranny. A doom of expiation laid on the sex, perhaps, for having been first in the transgression. Yet, tradition teaches also that through woman comes the redemption of humanity, and many earnest souls are even now waiting for some diviner revelation of the mission of woman than the world has yet seen. 'Earth waits for her Queen,' is the epigraph of Margaret Fuller's great essay, entitled, 'Woman in the Nineteenth Century.' As yet, however, the expiatory sacrifice goes on unchanged, and women still weep and toil, as they have ever done, that man, the lord of the world, may find

A

existence made easier and pleasanter by the ceaseless devotion and patient self-sacrifice of the inferior, at least, the weaker sex.

In the early ages, while men were warring or hunting, the women of the family performed all the servile duties; drawing water from the well, like Rebecca; tending the flocks, like Rachel; or cooking the food, like Sara, who was dismissed to knead cakes while angels were conversing with her husband.

Polygamy and slavery began even before Adam's death. 'Hear my voice, ye wives of Lamech,' exclaimed the dictatorial Antediluvian to his two wives, Adah and Zillah, who, no doubt, obeyed in silence, for their answers are not recorded in the sacred history.

Everywhere bondage was the portion of women. In the East they were considered as articles of traffic simply. A man acquired his rights over them just in proportion to his ability to purchase. Thus, Solomon had a thousand wives in his harem.

In Africa, women have ever been the hard-worked drudges of their barbarian masters. The three thousand and thirty-three wives of the King of Dahomey—to which mystic number he is limited—are but so many menials; and other African chiefs have a body guard formed of their young wives, to run beside their horses on state occasions.

But even in England, Christian England, the doom of the bond-slave is on the fated sex. For a true knowledge of the condition of women of the lower classes here, the revelations made by the Brothers Mayhew may be studied with profit; even in this splendid, wealthy London, the record is one long dreadful tragedy of toil and suffering, starvation and sin, under the sway and rule of their brutal masters.

Yet, occasionally women have risen by force of genius to stations of power and dignity, and proved themselves equal to the position, like Deborah, judge and prophet in Israel; or Semiramis, who built Babylon in one year; or the learned and beautiful Zenobia, who could be conquered only by an Aurelian; or the Carian Artemisia, whose statue was erected at Lacedemon.

But though rarely admitted to the Royal dignity, the office of the priesthood was often shared by women. For a very general belief existed as to their susceptibility to inspiration, and their peculiar relations with the spiritual world was part of the popular creed. All the great diviners of old were women—the Pythias

at Delphi; the Sybils; the Druidesses; the
Valkyria, and others; and this acknowledged
mysticism of woman was perhaps the origin
of the sacred respect shown to her in the East,
though politically she had no position. A
woman was required to be the symbol of stainless purity, and the nuptial rites were all framed
as types of this great virtue of chastity, which
was considered the basis of all others in the
female character.

The bath, whither the bride was conducted in
solemn procession, was the emblem of purification. The perfumes and jewels symbolised the
inner grace of the spirit; while the rose-
coloured bridal veil heightened and represented the blush of modesty; but the Jewish
writers say that the veil was worn because of
the angels; for it was the beauty of woman's
hair that tempted them down to love the
daughters of men.

And St Paul is supposed to allude to this
tradition when he says, ' A woman should
have a covering on her head, *because of the
angels.*'

A crown also was worn at the marriage, in
sign of the consecration to a higher life; hence
the Jews call a bride the ' The Crowned.' And
she was lifted over the threshold of her husband's

dwelling to signify that she entered it without stain.

In Syria the bride sits with closed eyes the first day of her arrival ; and a Bedouin girl remains blindfolded a week, to show that her husband is now a covering to her eyes. Purity is the one supreme virtue demanded of a woman, and if she fail in this, her husband has the power over her of life or death.

All exercise of intellect is discouraged in the East, except by performers for hire, and no man, even of the lowest class or caste, would marry a public dancer or singer, so degrading is held the exhibition of a woman's person or gifts, except for the one to whom she is consecrated.

The Buddhists, especially, maintain the divine right of the man over the woman ; for, according to the Hindu Shaster, the husband may divorce his wife if she scolds, or presumes to eat before he has finished his meal ; while in China a divorce can be obtained for loquacity, a tendency in women very prevalent amongst the Celestials ; for, says the Chinese proverb, 'What women have lost in their feet they have gained in their tongues.' Submission and industry are the chief virtues required of a Chinese wife. Even the Empress superintends the silk-winding and weaving, and the title of the chief court lady is 'The Mother of the Worms.' But female children are not allowed to over-crowd the Empire, so that it is customary to send round a cart every morning through the streets of Pekin to pick up dead babies of the baser sex.

Between the Black Sea and the Caspian, where the Aryan race had its origin, the perfection of human beauty is still to be found. Southward, from that centre, the type degenerates to the Ethiopian, and eastward to the Mongolian variety ; while northward the type still further degenerates to the flat-faced, square-headed, small-eyed Calmuch ; a mean and sinister-looking people, yet with intellect enough to hold women in bondage ; for the bride must pull off the husband's boots in token of submission, and a whip is given to him, which he scruples not to use.

In some tribes the bride is conveyed to her destined spouse with the touching rubric— ' Here, wolf, take thy lamb,' and baking utensils are buried with a woman, as bows and arrows with a man, so intensely allied do they consider the female soul and cookery.

The Javanese are a better specimen of the Mongolian race, for they permit women to divorce husbands at will; so that some women may even count up twenty husbands without having discovered one worth retaining. Still the fatal sign of degradation is exacted, for a bride is expected to wash her husband's feet as the first symbol of submission. One heroine, however, stands out in the Javanese annals an honourable example to her sex, for, having performed her portion of the ritual, she flung the water in the gentleman's face, and refused to accept him as her lord and master.

In Sumatra the taste in beauty is peculiar, and to please her lover a girl is required to flatten her nose, stretch her ears, and blacken her teeth; otherwise she would not be accepted as a wife. If she is unfaithful to her marriage vows, the punishment is to shave off her hair, while the lover, with summary justice, is eaten by the tribe.

In Borneo courage is supposed to win the heart of a woman; for no man takes a wife till he has cut off the head of an enemy. If he wishes a second wife he cuts off another head, and so on; wives and heads always equal.

If we now pass to New Holland, we find a frightful, ash-coloured race, greased, tattooed and scared; so hideous in appearance that ethnologists fail to trace their affinity to any of the existing human species. Still these hideous and degraded beings have attained, in one point at least, to the philosophy of civilisation, and fully uphold the supremacy of man over the woman. The marriage rites are simple, yet even more than symbolic, for the bride's front teeth are knocked out as a preliminary ; then the husband flings a kangaroo skin over her shoulders, and drives her before him to his hut with blows and hideous cries.

Ancient Egypt, however, combined, in a singular degree, the sensuous and the intellectual in the national treatment of women, for history records the names of many women who reigned and ruled there by learning and spiritual influence even more than by beauty. The principal deity was a woman, and the chief priestess of the Mysteries of Isis ranked next to the throne. Still, the worship of women was exceeded in sacred intensity by that of cats, for whom, if one happened to die, the whole family shaved the head in token of honour. But modern Egyptian women have now sunk into the usual routine of feminine life—love, dress and embroidery, and claim notice only by the excessive beauty of their eyes.

One grows weary of the woeful uniformity

of female life and bondage all over the world. Bought or sold for a handful of money at the Equator, or for a bottle of train oil at the Poles; everywhere degraded as slaves yet expected to have the virtue of saints, and to be the ministering angels of man's life.

In Madagascar, wives salute the husband by passing the tongue over his feet; and amongst the Moors, the wives stand and serve while their masters eat. Even the Esquimaux, who live upon tallow, and drink the blood of seals—a creature, half fish, and only half human —employs the small gleam of intellect vouchsafed to him in forcing his wife to become his bond-slave. Nothing, indeed, but the hypothesis that the fallen angels of Heaven are expiating their rebellion in the form of woman, can account for the universal humiliation of the fated race.

In Europe, although women have never had any proper political recognition, yet they have always exercised great social influence.

In early times the Greek women were allowed to vote in the public assemblies, and, though masculine jealousy still denied them equality as citizens, yet they had a permitted rivalry in all that evidenced the supremacy of mind.

Corinna would compete with Pindar in verse

and the daughter of Pythagoras lectured in his classes; Aspasia, the spirit queen of Pericles, discoursed philosophy to a listening Socrates; while maidens with that old desire for knowledge, for which Eve perilled Paradise, were known to disguise themselves as students to attend the lectures of Plato, although the ban of political inferiority was still resting on this sex.

In a land where the human form was a revelation of beauty, the religion, poetry; the rites, festivals; the language, music; where art had its noblest types, genius its brightest illustrations, and patriotism its immortal heroes, it is not strange that woman rose, through inspiration and sympathy, to be the priestess of intellect.

Therefore we find that the Greeks, above all, seem to have comprehended the true significance of women as the highest spiritual expression of humanity. The lofty and the beautiful, wisdom and grace, the secret harmonies of the universe, and the divine minor principle of nature were all symbolised under female forms, and their mythology was a true apotheosis of womanhood, free, however, from the bondage of marriage, for the muses and the divine Athené of the Parthenon were never married.

The Greeks evidently held that genius raises

woman to a lonely elevation. The priestess cannot at once tend the fire on the domestic hearth, and watch by the sacred flame on the Altar of God.

It is singular that although marriage is the only institution brought from Paradise, and dates its ritual from before the Fall, yet in no mythology is the idea of divine inspiration connected with it. Muse or sybil, priestess or pythoness, all on whom rested the spirit of prophecy or divination, belonged to the virgin class; and the vestals were honoured above all other women, as if by their mystic consecration to virginity, they became endowed with holier and higher powers.

At Rome the praetors and consuls lowered their fasces to them on the public way; a lictor attended them in the streets; they rode in chariots, and sat in the chief seats at spectacles in their white robes edged with purple, and the priestly fillet bound upon the brow, like the calm guardian genii of the empire, above and apart from all mere individual sympathies.

The position of women during the early period of European civilisation was not without dignity. The Gothic nations believed that amongst women many were endowed with the spirit of prophecy and mysterious powers over nature for good and evil. They were admitted to the priestly and legal offices, and sat at the war councils, and headed armies. Christianity developed this sense of woman's mystical nature into the chivalrous worship of the middle ages, where, through all the frenzied excesses of a courtesy gone mad, one can yet recognise the prevalent idea of woman's significance in the world as the inspirer, the spiritualiser, and the rewarder of the brave. The love of woman then ennobled like the love of glory. She was the high priestess of that religion of sentiment, honour and courage, that was the beautiful fanaticism of the creed of chivalry.

But the Pagan belief of her prophetic powers, and her half-deification by Christian chivalry, received further and fatal devolopment, till the notion finally gained ground that woman in some mysterious manner could form a league with Satan himself, and through his potent power exercise a terrible and malific influence over all things that excited her envy or her hatred. Then began the horrible persecutions that lasted throughout two centuries, when women, stigmatised as witches, were tortured, reviled, hunted down, burned alive, and stamped out of creation, if they had the fatal gift of more beauty, or more brains than other women.

After this terrible era the pretensions to supernatural power lay dormant for a long while until revived by the mesmerists, who brought forward startling proofs that women really had affinities with the spiritual world much stronger than exist in the other sex. And the strange, mystic power they evidently possess has now become an acknowledged fact in occult philosophy.

We have now traced the history of women from Paradise to the nineteenth century, and have heard nothing through the long roll of the ages but the clank of their fetters, some of iron, like the gyves of the African bond-slave; others perhaps of gold, like those of the captive Zenobia; or heavy with jewels, as the anklets of Odalisque; still fetters and manacles are on all; for law, prejudice and custom have combined to hold women in abject bondage for six thousand years.

One must regard, therefore, with genuine admiration the efforts of those brave-hearted heroines who, from time to time, have come forth from the ranks of the oppressed, and striven to interpret the true significance of woman in the idea of humanity, and to lift her from the bondage and low level of a narrow conventional code to the full perfection of a magnificent womanhood.

Yet there is still a mystery about woman's destiny which casts its shadow even over eternity. Here, the existence of woman is chiefly manifested by love and sacrifice, and patient self-abnegation, that others may rejoice ; heedless of herself, so as she can bring light to the life of those beloved. Thus she permeates all existence with sanctifying power, assuming all tenderest names and holiest relations—wife, mother, sister, daughter—so that under every form she may still—angel-like— stand beside man from the cradle to the grave, lavishing all that is beautiful in her nature with a silent devotion that exacts no return ; the heart her kingdom, the affections her ministers.

This is her apparent mission on earth, but in the life beyond, when these earthly ministrations are not needed, what will be the aim and meaning of her existence ? The position of the sex in the beatified universe is a sealed vision. Will male and female angels exist to all eternity, where there is no marrying or giving in marriage, or Cherubim and Seraphim, Knowledge and Love, are they, perchance, the male and female principle made eternally objective ; or is there a rotation for each soul by successive incarnations in male and female forms, until, at last, humanity attains some glorified, full-developed organisation, in which the special qualities of each sex will be united, the intellect and the love, the tenderness and the strength, or, least probable hypothesis of all, will our wondrous humanity, made higher even than the angels, be for ever divided into two races, one eternally lower than the other, so that, from first to last, the doom of woman may be read—subjection to man on earth, degradation beneath man in Heaven?

After all, perhaps, Swedenborg's visionary glance beheld the truth when he asserts that souls change sex at every moment in the spiritual world. Feminine when they aspire, masculine to the soul that has not yet reached an equal spiritual elevation, or as Emerson explains, 'You love the worth in me, then I am your husband; meanwhile, I adore the greater worth in another, and so become his wife. Do you love me, means, do you see the same truth? If so, we are happy, our souls blend in harmony; but, presently, one of us passes into the perception of higher truth, then we are divorced, no tension can hold us longer.'

This theory is confirmed by the fact that the love of woman is generally aspiration—hero-worship; while man receives homage more readily than he gives it.

It explains also the inconstancy of all-gifted, progressive natures; for such souls are for ever seeking new and loftier sympathies; therefore, the highest love is never mutual; the lower nature worships, but the higher still ascends and aspires.

Lastly, it explains the isolation of all genius; for the soul that yearns for the perfect, the infinite, the divine, cannot rest contented within the narrow limitations of one frail human heart inferior to it in all things. But justice to the women of earth is of more importance to us here than the destiny of women in Heaven, or speculations as to the rank they may hold in the future life. Enough if we demand and can obtain in this present span of time from law and usage, government and society, that woman hall have full privilege and freedom to develop all the powers of her intellect, as well as all the soft graces of her tender nature.

'What woman needs,' as Margaret Fuller observes, 'is not as a woman to rule, but as a nature to grow; as an intellect to discern; as a soul to lead the higher life, and unfold such power as were given her with the living breath of God on the day of creation.'

Hitherto, the chief dogma of woman's education has been simply husband-worship. She was taught that if she studied it was simply to qualify herself as a companion to her husband; if she talked, it should be just enough to show that she appreciated his profounder wisdom. She was to resign all individual taste, to dress only as he pleased, obey meekly as he ordered, and, whatever might be his faults, to give him unqualified homage as to a visible God.

It is time, surely, for this *Dalai Lama* religion to be somewhat modified; and already women are finding higher motives and nobler incentives for their life-work. Strong, redemptive souls have arisen amongst them to lead the crusade against custom and cant ; and soon some Jael may appear to break the political bondage, or a Judith the sensuous bondage in which the sex has been held, and through their efforts a new era may be given to the world of equal rights, equal culture, and equal honours for men and women.

It is remarkable that Christianity at once accepted woman as co-worker with man in the great mission of human elevation; and with what tenderness our Lord always treated the sex ! His first miracle was in honour of a marriage, and it was performed at the request of a woman. Twice for woman's tears He raised the dead to life ; His last human thoughts

B

were for a woman, and His first utterance from
the grave was to a woman. Even the humbled
sinner at His feet He raised from the dead
with the pardoning fiat,—' Neither do I condemn
thee ; go and sin no more.'

Yet the elevation that began by Christianity
has been only imperfectly carried out. In all
penal enactments, certainly, a stern equality
prevails, but all the social privileges of rank,
title, wealth, honours and position, are still
exclusively reserved for men.

Two moral codes even are framed for man
and woman, one permitting the widest latitude,
the other exacting the most rigid obedience,under
the penalty of being cast out into the wilderness.
Yet, while women are expected to be strong
against all temptation, no means are provided to
save them from the helpless poverty that so often
drags souls downward to despair. Nothing is
done by laws, government or 'society towards
giving women an honourable status and adequate reward for their gifts and work.

Yet many official positions might be selected
for which women would be fully competent.

Female professorships might be founded, lecturers appointed, each with a definite income,
and other and various paths of work and movement opened out to give women, not only the

means to live, but also a vivid interest in life by the honourable recognition of their gifts and powers. For this, too, is wanting to them, and the blank deprivation of all stimulants to exertion is fatal chiefly to women of genius ; and the atrophy of the soul that comes to them is often an agony harder to bear than even poverty with its bitter privations.

If men, destined for all the honours the world can give, yet often sink down weary under the burden of their work, how can women keep up a brave spirit without any prospect whatever of honour or reward. They who have to fight their way through closing icebergs of social prejudice, cant and sophisms, until, too often, the languor of hopeless effort succeeds the fitful and transient manifestations of the higher nature, and genius dies out in despair for want of a definite sphere of action and a suitable reward.

Recognition in some visible form is a healthful and natural stimulant to exertion ; for wherever there is talent there is ambition. Glory is the sympathy of the masses, and genius demands a shrine in the empire of humanity as well as an altar in the heart of one.

But in the freezing atmosphere of society what place have these consecrated souls of high intellect and impassioned sensibilities, mostly uncomprehended, always misunderstood.

They cannot rest contented in the dull monotony of daily cares, while every avenue to wealth and rank is carefully reserved by man for his own benefit, along with those symbols of honour which the crowd reverence, because significant of merit.

Men who fight, lawyers who plead, poets who sing, may receive the often well-earned title that lifts them to nobility, and symbolises the intellect that raised them above it ; but there is no peerage of talent for the gifted amongst women. They may run their chariots in the dust of a stadium, but never hope to wear the laurel crown.

The Queen has already founded an order for distinguished bravery, and even another order to reward the faithful services of her household servants ; would it not then be worthy of her sex and station to institute a royal order of merit for women eminent in literature and art, with title and life-income, after the ecclesiastical model—a peerage, in fact, without being hereditary.

Genius in man or woman deserves national recognition, of which rank and wealth are the outward and visible signs, and it is an injus-

tice to deprive half the nation of all chance
or hope of national honours, while equal taxation is imposed on all alike.

At present women assist in supporting every
institution of the empire, yet the Imperial taxes
never come back to them in any form of
benefit, and they are not even represented in
the legislature.

With men it is different, every station and
every honour is open for their competition, and,
if they are taxed, they benefit. But even if re-
presentation in Parliament be denied to women,
there might, surely, be an elective council of
representative women, to organise measures for
the advancement of the sex, and to formulate
their timid pleadings for justice into a resolute
demand.

The importance of special female universities should, above all, be advocated. Every
office to be held by women—as President,
Professors, and Lecturers—and each office to
be endowed with a certain definite rank and
income suitable to the attainments of the
recipient.

Female education at present is mere dilet-
tanteism. It does not give what women really
need so much, an assured status, and an honourable independence. They are allowed, cer-

tainly, at present, a limited access to the great universities, but all the profit and emoluments are still exclusively reserved for men.

Women, of course, if they have genius, can force their way into literature, but authorship is a very precarious profession, and seldom brings in an income on which life can be adequately supported ; besides, all may not have the gift. Many minds have capabilities for other manifestations of mental power, and a suitable sphere should be found for all. Action for some, reflective work for another. Some souls speak best in deeds, in a life of rule and influence. Let such women be given stations of power and dignity—colonial government, for instance. Why not vice-queens as well as queens ? Any station where intellect can be evidenced by a life of energetic good might be given to women thus gifted. To others leave the symbol of speech, and let the lonely spirit fashion it into a lever to move the world's great heart. The passionate pleadings of women for a due share of the rank and honours of the empire cannot always be stifled with the phrase :—' Independent women, learned women, thinking women, are not liked ; society only wants pretty, well-dressed women to attract and amuse.' And so, many a fine intellect amongst women lies buried under the dessicating social system, like some grand statue of a god beneath the Libyan sands.

Yet, there is no greater fallacy than the doctrine that women should be mere negations if they desire to charm and please in society ; for ignorance and shallow vanity soon weary, even though aided by the the glamour of beauty. And no woman without intellect ever yet gained permanent influence over a man's life.

'If women,' says Addison, 'would but think as much of the adornment of their minds as of their persons earth would soon recognise her queen.'

As the old Greek mythus teaches—It is the Cestus of Venus that confers the real power of fascination, for it means spiritual grace ; and without it even Venus herself failed to captivate. Genius never yet unsexed a woman, or learning or culture ever so extended ; but the meanness of her ordinary social, routine life, with all its petty duties and claims, and ritual of small observances, degrades and humiliates her, for it deprives her of all dignity, and leaves her without any meaning in God's great universe.

Hear how a modern poet mourns over female inanity and woman's 'drossy chat' with the silly homage of silly lovers :—

'Still as before and as now, balls, dances, and evening parties,
Shooting with bows, going shopping together, and
hearing them singing ;
Dangling beside them, and turning the leaves at the
dreary piano ;
Utter divorcement from sense, mother earth, and
object of living.'

While with rude eloquence he denounces
the indolent vanity of woman's purposeless
life :—

' Ye unhappy statuettes, ye miserable trinkets,
Poor alabaster chimney-piece ornaments under
glass cover ;
Come in God's name, come down. The very
French clock by you
Puts you to shame with its ticking; the fire-irons
deride you ;
Come in God's name, come down ! Do anything ;
be but something! '

This is the true gospel needed for women,—
' Be but something!' A life of noble aims is a
life of truest beauty—a music manifested. For
the whole being then moves harmoniously forward in an ascension toward the highest and the
divine.

Women of intellect, especially, cannot accept
the routine life of ordinary society and be happy.
They revolt against the claims on time and

thought of our petty conventional usages; they refuse to accept the limitations imposed by society on freedom of action; they chafe in the fetters of prejudice; and their strong, passionate natures spring up elastic against the injustice of laws and the bondage of social fictions. There are some brows that will not bend to be seared with the brand of inferiority, some souls that will not be fused into the uniform conglomerate demanded of mediocrity, like rocks in the lava stream its fires even cannot calcine. They demand a higher platform on which to plant the banner of the rights of women, with all the aids that society, the world, the universe can give to ensure the intellectual advancement of their sex.

Meanwhile woman need not be taken from the circle of her womanly duties, which are also her holiest joys; for all the triumphs of intellect fail to give her perfect happiness unless she is centered likewise in a strong, loving heart.

The praise of crowds, the glare of applause, never yet adequately compensated for the low, approving voice of one, and human love must thrill through every fibre of her being, or life, even in the splendour of success, would be to her but a twilight Urania without sunshine or glow.

Love is truly the sacrament of life by which consecrated souls rise into a diviner strength; yet it is still but a type of the higher aspirations for which the soul was created, and which alone can fill the spirit's infinite capacity for ascension and adoration.

Human relations, however, will adjust themselves without intervention of preachers or laws. They are the palm trees in the wilderness, beneath which the soul rests instinctively a space in its onward journey, a transient shadow, not an abiding home, while around rolls the cycle of eternity, and above is God, the true Bridegroom of the Soul.

Yet, surely, the sanctifying influences of human love will not be lessened because nobler existences meet within the limit of its many blessings. The highest minds are ever the holiest lovers. Wisdom and knowledge will not annihilate human passion, but rather bring down on it a diviner spirituality to sublimate and purify the earthly and the sensuous.

But some women, perhaps, may still pine in the mere limits guarded by the penates; proud, inspired souls, who need the world for a sphere, humanity for an object, and the glory of sacrifice for some great cause more than all the soft pleasures of domestic love. These, too, will find their place at last, when every portal is opened to woman's intellect. They will become spiritual leaders of light and progress, and need no longer stand lonely in life, like a star rent from its system. Some noble purpose, some grand sphere, where passionate energy can work along with duty, will ensure for these lofty missionary natures the only happiness of which such exalted organisations are susceptible.

Thus, every grade and class, thinkers and doers, apostles of freedom or ministrants of mercy, will manifest after their ability the divine uses of existence, and claim their right as women to a recognised place amongst the workers for humanity.

GENIUS AND MARRIAGE.

ALPHONSE DAUDET, the brilliant French
novelist, maintains in his clever work, 'Les
Femmes d'Artistes,' that the marriage state is
quite detrimental to the highest intellectual
life, and mars its development. Not that he
speaks from the experience of his own home,
for his wife is a brilliant, handsome woman,
holds her station with distinguished success,
and is quite worthy to be the wife of a celebrity;
while Daudet himself has none of that severe
dogmatism which makes nervous people tremble
in the presence of intellect; he is handsome and
fascinating, with beautiful eyes and perfect
manners. But such marriages, where life glides
on in graceful calm without a discord or the
crash of opposing temper, are rare and exceptional. The rule remains that complete isolation
from small domestic cares, perfect freedom from
all social routine, is absolutaly necessary for
those peculiar natures in which the tumultuous

elements of genius are always striving toward
some visible organic expression.

'No solitude, no glory,' should be the epigraph
over the sacred adytum where the priesthood of
intellect celebrate their mysteries. And, with
this passion for solitude strong in him, Daudet,
when first entering on the literary career, fled
from the glare of Paris pleasures and took up
his abode for months in the weird solitude of a
lighthouse, on an island rock off the coast of
Corsica, holding communion only with the winds
and the waves and the rushing tempest of his
own emotions. It is from his own knowledge
of the artist nature that he draws his arguments
against marriage, while his illustrations are
taken from the intellectual circles of Paris which
he knows so well, and where many a man of
genius has had his nerves shattered and his life
ruined by the mistake of an ill-assorted union.

A poet friend, with whom he discusses the
subject one evening at the hour *des effusions et
des confidences*, maintains the contrary opinion,
and gives Victor Hugo as an example of the
highest genius, whose life was made still more
radiant by the soft charm of domestic ties.

Precisely, replies his opponent, because he is
the highest type. Victor Hugo is not a man,
but humanity—a nature made up of all natures.

He is never led; he dominates all influences, and bends them into pliant instruments, from which his soul draws music. But the artist who is not superhuman like Victor Hugo, should beware of bondage to the emotions. He should stand apart from all human ties in order that he may more calmly analyse the workings of passion. His mission is to reveal the hidden mysteries of the soul, and, for the furtherance of philosophical analysis, he may even break a heart, but should never allow his own to be weakened by combat with inferior natures.

All writers who have studied life teach the same doctrine. Edmond About says that a man of genius should close the book of love after the prologue; for, if he gives his heart wholly to a woman, she returns it to him broken.

For true spiritual natures pine in bondage. All routine of law and conventionalism is hateful and revolting to them. Their lives have no fixed orbit. They alternate in phases of ecstasy and agony, in storms and whirlwinds, or the gloom of a midnight despair; and for these beings of nerves and caprices a special type of women should be created; but the world seldom affords an example of such a type.

The daughters of men who wed with the sons of the gods, should have courage to face the lightnings and the thunders, if they dare to stand on the mountain height with an immortal husband. For such a man, and to insure his happiness, a woman should be ready to give her life with sublime self-immolation. At once an angel and a victim, sensitive to every chord of his nature, yet with a smile forever on the lip, no matter what anxieties may corrode the heart.

Genius is an exotic that requires to be nursed in sunshine, but the ordinary, common-place wife too often chills and blights the divine spirit through her shallow egotism, forever exacting, never giving ; estimating work only, as Daudet says, by its money value ; therefore she teases her husband to make busts of mediocrities, because they generally pay well, and to paint the faded, affected women of society, because it may bring him into fashion. And she insists on his going out with her, as she likes to be noticed as the wife of a celebrity. To all this the husband generally consents in a meek, submissive way ; for, except in moments of passionate inspiration when the god descends on him, the artist is the weakest creature under heaven, so easily led and duped by a woman tyrant.

But some day he violently breaks the bonds, and a scene, a fracas, a separation is the result. Alphonse Daudet draws such a picture from life. The world says of the husband, 'How wicked of him to leave his wife, such an excellent woman, so active in her house, everything so orderly, and she never left him for a moment.'

Exactly, there was the horror of it. She never left him. He pined for solitude in those precious moments of intellectual excitement, when thought is organised to form only in divine stillness; but he never could attain it. She was there, always there, arranging and settling, methodical and punctual and orderly; abounding in all those virtues that kill great thoughts; incapable of sympathy, and entirely failing to comprehend the needs and peculiarities of the sensitive temperament of genius. So he fled. His life was wrecked, but his soul was liberated, and he was content. Solitude and liberty are for artists and gods.

Ill-assorted marriages torture the gifted in many other ways. The musician finds that his wife has no ear for music, and she always begins to chat with her friends, or declaim loudly to her refractory servants, when his soul is going forth into the infinite, and his hand 'loosens the notes in a golden shower.'

The poet's wife generally hates poetry, calls it ' stuff,' and laments that her husband cannot write, like other people, paragraphs and acrostics or prize parodies that bring in such quantities of money.

Even love marriages have no sure foundation in the intellectual temperament. To see, love and wed in a moment is ecstatic ; but to live and not love for the whole after-term of human existence is a fearful reality, too often experienced, in all its dull depression, when unrelated souls are bound together by the irrefragable marriage chain.

A young writer of promise and rising fame sees a pretty shop-girl, a jeweller's daughter, and is fascinated at once. She was so gentle and insinuating, so charming, with her little curled head and her little white hands, daintily fingering the glittering trinkets, and her placid smile that always beamed a welcome. He fancies that under her rule the disorder of his bachelor home will be changed to a paradise of comfort, and they are married. But the sunshine came not ; only a grey, watery atmosphere of fog seemed to envelop his life. When his clever friends came as usual, and thought flashed as at a Platonic symposium, the wife sat by and smiled her placid smile,

and uttered the small platitudes of mediocre
natures, the set colloquial phrases of commerce,
with the most exasperating unconsciousness
that she was a bore and wearisome to them
all. On the contrary, she fancied she was
quite an addition to the circle, so nice, lady-
like and well bred.

Then the horror of a dreadful truth fell upon
the husband's heart. He became conscious that
he would have to sit opposite to this woman
and look at her vapid smile, and listen to her
flimsy talk, for, perhaps, half a century. There
was no help for him. No release. Sometimes
the tumult of his feelings raged in open war, and
then she wept and lamented that she had not
married one or other of the young shopmen who
were dying about her, and were now so well off.

But after a time matters grew worse. She
began to assume airs as the wife of an author,
to give her opinion, and interrupt the conversation with her affected gush of praise. The
husband could see the suppressed laughter on
the lips of the Platonists, and their contempt
for the little fool he had made his wife. This
finished his agony. He gave up his friends.
He gave up writing, fell into a state of morbid
melancholy, and finally died, leaving all his precious manuscripts confused and incomplete. The

widow crammed them all into the fire, smiled as before, and eventually married one, or, perhaps, both of the admiring shopmen. And she still utters her little platitudes of commerce, and refers, as to a martyrdom, to her first marriage with that poor scribbler who never could earn enough by anything he wrote to keep her in proper style.

But if the small common-place mind is exasperating, perhaps the untamed freedom of the half savage, the fearless passions of a daughter of the people, would suit the requirements of the exceptional soul of genius.

So thought a young French artist as he looked on the· massive figure, the heavy coils of black hair, the grand limbs of a superb Tranteverine, as she stood in the mud of the shallows fishing for eels. How splendid she was in the flashing sunlight, with her great eyes, her scarlet bodice, her white chemisette tucked up high over the great sculptural arms, and then her mad, merry laughter that stirred the air like a rush of the breeze through the pine woods. He made a picture of her at once, which excited immense admiration at the Exposition. A glorious study of sky and air, and the full rich life of youth, in a flush of colour and a glow of light.

At last he had found an ideal to take into
his life. He hated the false affected woman of
society, but here was a beautiful savage, a child
of the sun and the storms and the flowers;
she would give his artist life eternal youth—so
he married her. She had no possession save a
big red cat, and he carried her and the cat to
Paris.

But when she put on the Paris dress like
other people, what a mournful transformation
of the daughter of the sun. A great splendid
animal in a little Paris bonnet, always tilting to
one side over the heavy masses of hair was a
failure, and the great Roman feet, made for
splashing in the reeds and the rushes, limped
sadly in the little Paris boots, and the effect of
a Paris mantle on the great broad shoulders
was altogether deplorable. Even her beauty
seemed to have disappeared with the loss of her
native picturesque surroundings. Then her coarse
language, her large gestures, her bad French,
all these things agonised him at every moment.
A savage veneered is an artistic mistake.

He saw it all and sighed, and withdrew from
the world where he could never bring a wife
who talked as loud in society as if she were
hailing a boat across the Tiber, and whose
laugh shook the room like an earthquake.

However, they have got over ten years of married life. The heavy chin, the broad shoulders, the vulgar mouth, have become accentuated; still the eyes are splendid, and the artist - husband has learned to endure a good deal. She is so good-hearted and kind though when she claps him on the back, and presses him to eat some dish which she has spent all the morning preparing, he shudders, and a silent aspiration rises to his lips that he had left her on her own soil amid the reeds and the rushes, with her cat and the eels and the fishermen of the Tiber.

Other experiences in married life have proved equally uncongenial to the strange, sensitive, artistic nature. A young dramatist, with eyes of fire and soul of flame, fancies he will find his ideal in the first love of a pure young heart—a simple, docile girl, that he can mould as he chooses by his strong will, and breathe, as it were, a divine spirit into the clay.

'Yes,' he said to his friend, 'I liked her clear innocent eyes, her calm expression that no passions had ever disturbed; even her little provincial accent and ways I liked, for they suggested the pure innocence of the country life.

'And now to say that I hate her accent; I

hate her ways; I hate this torpid soul that no effort of mine can wake to life or sensibility. I read my poem to her—my great, noble poem. "How pretty," she said, and yawned.

'I could have killed her. But I was calm, and explained to her that poetry was the highest expression of the divine, and that she ought to strive to comprehend its depth and meaning. She smiled as if I were an idiot, and said she liked common sense, but what I read seemed all nonsense. Common sense, the instinct of common brains and cold hearts.

'She cared nothing for music, nor for art, nor even for dress, only for good solid household work, and economies above all. When our clever circle discussed art and literature with their usual fervent vehemence, she sat silent, stuck up in a corner at her eternal needlework, and looked on with such a contemptuous sneer that my friends began to hate the sight of her, and gave up their visits. Then she brought in her own set. Oh, heavens! The bathos of these mediocre souls, the torture of listening to the shallow talk of commonplace women. Can you wonder that I left her? The influence of a nature like hers on a man's intellect is like a slow poison. And why should I allow my soul to be slowly murdered by a woman, merely because she is called my wife? No, I tried honestly to lift her to my level, but she would not be lifted.

'So the horrible dream is over, and I am free. These obstinate, self-opinionated women, without sympathy or the power to appreciate, are a dull leaden weight on life; besides, she was not happy with me, and we are better parted.'

It is quite true that the temperament and ways of literary men are often very irritating to a woman, their disorder and recklessness, their utter want of a law of life, sometimes sitting up all night, or lying in bed all day or for days together, to finish an essay or a drama undisturbed, the atmosphere of cigars they live in, the fever and the fret, the sleeplessness and the stimulants, and their intense, ingrained, though unconscious selfishness, these things none but a woman nobly resolved to be a victim can endure. Yet the temperament only is to blame, the man never means to be unkind, or to make his wife walk on ploughshares. The artisan can work at all times with perfect freedom, but genius can only work in moments, in fits and spasms, when the idea must be caught flying, or it will come no more, and in these tempestuous moments of cerebral

excitation the path must be left free for the
rush of the chariot wheels, and all the home life
must be hushed into a fearful silence lest the
inspiration should be disturbed before the word
of power has been uttered.

Then there are days of weird, wordless gloom,
when a large parcel lies on the table, ' Declined
with thanks,' and the wife knows it is there,
like the corpse of a murdered innocent, but
cares not to allude to it, only its presence is felt
by the sombre silence that pervades the house,
and the fitful temper at the dinner-table of the
husband.

To some women the reflected glory of being
the wife of a celebrity compensates for the
actual discomfort, but unless a woman can
accept immolation cheerfully, she becomes
miserable herself, and a hindrance in place of
a helpmeet to her husband. There is also the
constant difficulty of getting money when there
is no regular income, and one has to live on
capital evolved from the brain in some happy
fit of working power. And when money comes
in, how recklessly it is spent! What ceaseless
subscriptions for statues, tombs and memorials
to the deceased brotherhood of genius. And
what endless efforts to found a new ' literary
review' which is to take the world by storm,

always the craze of a young band of writers,
though generally ending in failure, bitterness
and bankruptcy.

Naturally, and by instinct, a woman has a
strong tendency to look on a man of genius
as a god, and to offer him worship as well as
love; but in the fatal intimacy of daily life
illusions soon vanish, and she finds that, except in moments of inspiration, her divinity is
even weaker than an ordinary mortal, less able
to guide or strengthen others; so she resents
the knowledge that her idol is only made of
clay, and her feelings alternate between contempt and dislike, especially if she is of a
passionate, impulsive temperament.

An excellent man, an horticulturist, the head
of a nursery garden, had a wife of this description — handsome, ardent, and about ten
years his junior. Amidst her beautiful flowers
in the silent garden she dreamed of the Paris
world of splendour and celebrities, where even
she also might reign as a queen, and be ad-
mired and flattered, were she only seen and
known. Then the dream would vanish, and
she saw only the bowed down back of her
respectable husband over his flowers, and heard
only the snipping of the hedges and the eternal
drip of the watering-pot; and she wearied sadly

over the gravel walks, the mathematical beds,
the geometrical exercise, and the life regulated
by the barometer.

So the years passed till she reached the
trente ans — the fatal age when passion becomes reckless in the despair of vanishing youth.

Just then a poet arrives in the little provincial town, and is provincially lionised. A true
poet of the *salons*, with cavernous eyes, floating hair, and a pale, sombre, fatal face. He
is always perfectly dressed. No lyric disorder
apparent, save in the somewhat careless tie
of his cravat.

Everyone invited him ; he always came late,
between ten and midnight, and it was an im-
pressive thing to see him as he leaned upon
the mantelpiece, tossed back his long hair,
and spoke, as if in a melancholy dream, of
the soul of the poet tortured by passion and
despair. But the excitement was at its height
when he declaimed his celebrated poem, ' The
Creed of Love,' beginning with the stupendous
line,—

' I believe in Love as I believe in God.'

And all the pretty women in their full evening
dress gathered round, and gazed at him with
earnest, humid eyes.

Of course, the wife of the respectable horticulturist was vanquished at once. What woman
of unfulfilled aspirations, whose husband only
snipped and planted and watered, could resist
the magic influence of this Orphic revelation?

After a few interviews she flung herself at
the poet's feet, and declared that life was no
longer endurable with 'this man' (on these
occasions the husband is always 'this man,'
even though he is a scientific gardener).

The poet was rather embarrassed by the gift
of her devotion, but he could not refuse, so they
departed together for Paris.

Now, she thought, the reign of intellectual
splendour will begin ; but how different was the
reality. A mean apartment, a moody, irritable
companion ; no brilliant world waiting to receive
her with homage and admiration. On the contrary, society treated her with the most super-
cilious impertinence, and she was left to an
ignoble solitude, while the poet, faultlessly
dressed, went out every evening and declaimed
' The Creed of Love' to other women, the elegant and fashionable women of society, who
disdained to notice her existence. But even this
might have been borne could she still have worshipped ; but she found her idol querulous and
fretful, hypochondriacal and abominably selfish.

He was always imagining he was ill, and the table was covered with vials and powders, and the room kept at stove heat. What a change after her garden and the flowers and the pure air!

After a month or so of broken illusions, life became insupportable to her. She was stifled in the atmosphere of the close room, wearied with his temper, and she began to hate 'The Creed of Love.' How to escape was now her only thought. At length she wrote to her husband, told him all, entreated him to come for her. She had outlived her dreams, and would now be a good wife to him henceforth and for ever.

He was a philosopher; he forgave, and he came. One evening, while the poet was declaiming 'The Creed of Love' at an assembly of worshipping women, she left the house, found her excellent husband waiting with a carriage at the end of the street, and the midnight train whirled her back to peace, order, her beautiful gardens, and a happy, rational life. For, after all, a rational husband is the best companion for the life-long marriage state. The poet lover, with his moods and caprices, was only endurable when a glamour of glory covered him like a silver veil; and the veil, we know, is thrown on merely for society, and is never worn in the dull routine of common every-day life.

But it must be confessed that women have often many and grievous faults in married life, very irritating to a literary husband and a man of genius. And the philosopher of antiquity, who would not raise his eyes for three years, lest they should rest upon a woman, had, no doubt, suffered from some woman's aggravating ways while he was trying to devote himself to the abstractions of philosophy.

Their chief fault is a childish jealousy of a man's life work, manifested in overt acts of ill-temper, and other modes of annoyance. This is the common failing of common minds. A woman has torn the canvas from the easel where her husband was at work in a fit of jealous rage. Another, with grim determination, always chose the time when the author sat down to write to practise her scales or pound at some terrible sonata. And one (though such cruel malignity is scarcely credible) has been even known to hum a tune in the very room where her poet husband was striving to finish a beautiful and elaborate sonnet. And all this out of spite and jealousy for some fancied neglect.

The best chance, perhaps, of domestic felicity is when all the family are Bohemians, and all clever, and all enjoy thoroughly the erratic, impulsive, reckless life of work and glory, indifferent to everything save the intense moments of popular applause.

Such a family may be met in the art circles of Paris. The mother had been a model and a beauty, and still posed as Hebe when she handed a cup of tea to a visitor. The daughters, handsome, brilliant and clever, as the children of artists always are, sing, act, recite, dance, dress better than anyone else. Everything looks picturesque on them. Fashionable ladies vainly desire the pattern of that flowing train, that lifted robe, that classic sleeve; but no pattern is to be had. All was arranged by the aid of a few pins in the caprice of the moment as the handsome girls chatted and laughed before the mirror in their little room. Youth, beauty, and artistic taste can work wonders with the most chaotic materials.

People asked how they managed to pay for everything; but they never paid. That was their magic secret.

Bills, of course, were endless; but when some particularly severe creditor appeared, one of the splendid daughters pleaded with such a bewitching smile that he would 'call next Monday' (it was the family formula), that he retired humbled

and abashed from the glorious presence, as if
his claim had been an impertinence.

There was no regular dinner hour. A kind
of gipsy camp was held behind the screen, and
nourishment was taken with lawless haste during the transition intervals of the drama of
life.

When a good sum came in for a picture by
the father, they spent it right royally; not,
indeed, paying the School Board or the water
rate, or the consolidated house taxes—such
things depress genius—but in some splendid
outlay of extravagant revelry, which kept them
in high spirits for a week after, and they worked
all the better for it.

The State, surely, ought to consider the importance of preserving genius from low cares;
and Parliament might pass a bill to exempt
the race of the gifted from taxation. For these
brilliant beings are necessary to the world;
they supply the life, the phosphorus, the divine
fire, the grace, beauty, and charm of existence,
and the nation in return should relieve them
from all the mean burdens of prosaic and
parochial claims.

The true joy of the artist is in work; and
when every member of the family has a special
gift, which is repaid by the world's praise, then

everyone is happy. There is no idleness, no *ennui*. No one throws the burden of his life on another, no one needs a victim ; all work and all triumph, and learn to live and reign alone. Even when youth has passed, artistic instincts still give grace and joy to life, and the world still continues its homage to the abdicated royalties of genius.

The more independent of each other each member of the household is, the greater the chance of happiness. If every wife had a definite employment, she would be less given to those little jealousies and watchings and pryings that fill up the time of vacant minds. An American writer has said, ' The great mistake in female education is making the possession of a husband the first consideration in place of only the second.' The life-work should be the first ; and the life-work need not hinder the beautiful ministrations of love, but it will make a woman stronger and nobler, more ready to pardon and help in moments of trial.

Unhappily, it is seldom that two equal and eternally related souls meet in the marriage state ; but this age has given an example of at least one such divine marriage, when the great poet wedded the great poetess of England in bonds of mutual love and honour. No jealousy was possible, for each stood on the supreme height of fame, and no cares or troubles marred the flow of genius in a married life, made radiant by fortune, luxury, art, culture, travel, high social position, and the world's applause. Death made the memory of this union sad and sacred, but the love remained to the last; and the poet's genius gave it life and light. The most beautiful verses in Mr Browning's latest volume are consecrated to a thought of her who shared the glory of his life, and to an aspiration for their reunion.

Mrs Carlyle failed to reach happiness because she had ambition without fame, and intellect without a career, and was too self-conscious and proud to be content with a subordinate part in life. She ought to have considered that her existence was really of no importance to the universe; but, her husband's words and works had power to send the world on its path of progress with mighty tangential force, and to drive a current of new life into the heart of the century. He was necessary to humanity; but she was only necessary to smooth the path his soul travelled. In this line of duty lay the beautiful mission of a loving wife, and in this she ought to have found happiness; but she only thought of the small annoyances that lay

D

in her own path, and pronounced herself 'miserable'—though holding the proud position of wife to the greatest man of the age! Yet she loved him as well as her nature would permit; but egotism can never nobly worship nor see the glory through the mist, and all the trials that made her 'miserable' resulted more from faults in her own disposition than from her husband's temper.

Had she married the village schoolmaster she might have been happier. A keen, clever, homely Scotchwoman, with her sharp tongue and her broad Scotch accent, she would have ruled the parish admirably. And this should have been her destiny; but Carlyle raised her to eminence as his wife, gave her station and dignity in the great capital of the world; and in return she darkened his fame, gave his name to the scoffers, and chilled the enthusiasm that would have raised memorials to his honour.

From the woman that stands beside the man of genius in life much is demanded. She is the angel of his destiny, and accountable to the world for the treasure committed to her care— the peace and serenity of his soul. Some men work, and the world crowns them—they have their recompense; others work and die in their youth, and the world weeps for them; but some work and suffer, and the world neither crowns nor weeps. For them, at least, let a woman live, or, if need be, let a woman die. The one supreme grace for the wife of a man of genius is the grace of immolation and self-sacrifice.

A woman is so easily replaced in the vast working world of life, but a great man's throne is vacant for evermore. Yet it must be remembered that under no circumstances can genius be made happy. The artist nature burns with an infinite desire for the infinite that nothing earthly can satisfy. Happiness is for the commonplace only — for the mechanical workers to whom success means wages, not glory. A victim upon whom can be laid all the burden of existence is needed by the high priest of genius, and a wife may not have the sacrificial vocation. Hence the sum of all experience is apparently rather against marriage for the race of the gifted ; but the question still remains undecided. No new arguments have been adduced, and nothing stronger has been said on the subject by any modern writer than what Milton uttered two hundred years ago, when he wrote his celebrated treatise to prove that the loneliest life was better than an unsuited marriage, when two persons without any spiritual affinity were bound together in irrevocable bondage by the words of a ritual, 'to their unspeakable weariness and despair,' and life became to them, in Milton's expressive words, 'a drooping and disconsolate household captivity, without refuge or redemption.'

SOCIAL GRACES.

BEAUTY is generally considered as the most seductive and irresistible of social graces. Yet even beyond the fascination of beauty may be ranked the charm of manner, and the brilliant interchange of thought between refined and cultivated intellects. Manner may indeed take the first place amongst social gifts, for it has an ethical value as a refining influence in all grades of life. It promotes harmony, softens ascerbity of temper, and diffuses a calm joy over the home circle ; while in society it dominates as no other gift or grace can do. Beauty may often have fatal power to draw souls earthward, and conversation, with all its wit and brilliancy, may be used to vitiate the moral sense; but manner is ever noble and ennobling, because based on the two great moral principles, respect for oneself and respect for others. Christianity has formulated this harmonising principle in the words, ' As ye would that men should do to you,

do ye also to them,' and the positivist philosophy
calls it 'Altruism,' as opposed to selfishness and
egotism, the very qualities most atagonistic to
fine and noble manners. Manner exists as an
heirloom amongst some races, as the Celt, the
Slav and the Arab. The courtesy of the Celt
approaches reverence, and the Bedouins have
the calm majesty of desert kings. All the
Latin races generally have singular grace of
idiom and gesture, but the Teuton is naturally
uncouth and rough. Mr John Bright, in one of
his eloquent addresses to working men, said with
truth, that 'manners, far more than pomp and
luxury, form the chief difference between high
and low, rich and poor, the noble and ignoble,
and if the working classes could be trained into
habits of mutual courtesy and politeness, if they
were made sensible of the moral beauty of good_
ness, forbearance, self-respect and reverence,
there would be less of the hideousness of coarse
language and brutal self-assertion in their
ordinary intercourse.' Manner is a royal grace
that we are accustomed to associate with high
rank and high breeding, but it may dwell in the
cottage as in the palace, and it has this advantage, that, while it can beautify all life, it costs
nothing, and never generated an evil thought or
word. The true science of manner is in the

nature and heart, in the sensitive insight into another's feelings, and the instinct which avoids all that could hurt or wound, combined with the readiness to give honour where honour is due. But training and cultivation are still very necessary to bring the outward gesture into accordance and harmony with the inward grace. The voice must be taught modulation, the intonation brought to the perfection of clear and sonorous music, and the eyes, the lips, the hands, all made to express emotion with dignity and grace. Mr Matthew Arnold says that the proper training of the muscles of the mouth would alone be sufficient to make a people beautiful, and redeem the lowest type from utter ugliness, for the sin of a vulgar face lies chiefly in the helpless, inexpressive mouth. It is the charm of the French mouth, with its ever-varying curves, that gives such intelligence and expression to the French face. Then the language is labial, and that in itself helps to form a fine expressive mouth, with full command over the muscles, hence, *le sourire spirituelle de France* has become celebrated. There is therefore a deep truth underlying the very amusing 'prunes, prism and poetry,' recommended to young ladies entering a room, for in reality labial sounds should be selected and adopted in conversation in pre-

ference to the sibilant and guttural, which
distort the mouth and destroy facial harmony.
The French look so well talking that they are
fond of it; indeed, Balzac assures us that in
Paris alone is found the spontaneous, graceful
intelligence of manner from which springs all
good conversation.   There is, in truth, a won-
derfully seductive grace in voice, tone, intonation
and movement, yet how little are they cultivated.
These exquisite charms are almost wholly left
to the professional artists, who consequently
rule mankind by their fascination.   Yet it would
be quite possible to make every woman as
perfect in tone and gesture as a trained actress.
Everyone cannot be taught to sing or paint, but
they all may be taught to speak clearly, intonate
musically, and to move with dignity and grace.
A year's training at the Dramatic College should
be considered indispensable to every girl's education.   Why, asks a French writer, cannot *Les
gestes gracieux, la tournure elegante* of the stage,
the noble movements of the head, the hands and
arms, and the cultivated voice, be brought into
our ordinary social life.   The voice alone has an
infinite power to charm; yet of all graces it is
the most neglected.   The Greeks fully recognised the importance of manner and voice, and
their children were early trained in habits of

politeness and graceful courtesy. The youths were made to recite Homer, to gain command of sonorous language and rhythmical cadence ; they were taught to move to music, to maintain a noble dignity of bearing, easy grace, a low and level tone, and never to degenerate to laughter.

Their great philosophers, Pericles, Plato, and Aristotle, were models of fine manners ; and the noble description given by Aristotle of the demeanour suited to a perfect gentleman, might be studied with advantage in the highest circles of nineteenth century civilisation. St Paul, who was deeply versed in Greek philosophy, had no doubt also studied the Greek code of manner. Coleridge notices the perfect courtesy and high breeding of St Paul, of which a notable instance is his reply to King Agrippa, 'I would that thou and all who hear me were even as I am, *except these bonds.*' Here was the courage of his creed skilfully combined with the deference due to royal rank. The perfect grace and noble dignity of this answer could not be surpassed. In the rush of modern life the old elaborate forms of social etiquette are rapidly dying out. Visiting is carried on through the penny post, correspondence by the telegraph, and conversation by the telephone. Science is killing all the stately grace of life, and flings so many treasures to society, that the Beautiful, like Tarpeia, is crushed to death under the weight of the offerings.   Machinery, railroads, telegraphs and cheap literature have destroyed beauty, grace, style, dignity and the art of conversation. Aristotle's high-bred gentleman, with his stately manners, slow movements and measured speech, would be soon hustled aside at a railway station, and probably lose his place and his ticket. Neither has society any longer the time to listen, as it did half a century ago, to the learned disquisitions of Macaulay, the inspired monologues of Coleridge, or the fierce-rolling iconoclastic thunders of Carlyle. The art of conversation has been gradually falling into decadence, and now barely exists ; though manner, or the mode of saying things well, still helps to keep it alive and even to give to common-places the semblance of gold.   In Shakespeare's time conversation was perhaps at its best in England.   The Court set the example ; Queen Elizabeth had wit and learning, and round her circled some of the most remarkable men that England or Europe ever produced.   Culture had reached a high level, and everyone aimed at being clever and brilliant, and above all, learned.   It was the golden age of England when the national intellect reached its supreme height in philosophy, poetry, the drama, and the splendour and depth of thought in social life. Queen Anne, though the dullest of good women herself, was fortunate also in having her reign illustrated by a great race of intellectual celebrities, all of them eminently distinguished for conversational power, as Swift, Pope, Bolingbroke, Lady Mary Wortley Montagu, and others. And there were great and brilliant women talkers even in the heavy Georgian era, whose wit and wisdom are preserved to us in the bright pages of Horace Walpole, like dried rose-leaves, with the perfumes still fragrant as in life. Dr Johnson is the high priest of the last century, and we fling a wreath to the memory of the fascinating Thrale, and 'little Burney,' and the wonderful and learned Mrs Delany, and the stately Hannah More, and others who proved woman's right to be a social queen. After them comes a whirlwind of intellect, male and female, rushing down the dark unknown of the opening nineteenth century. Immortal names of immortal men illustrate this great era, and a whole host of brilliant women light it with the radiance of their intellect, their wit, their beauty, and the sparkling splendour of their conversational gifts. Maria Edgeworth held the sceptre of intellect,

Lady Morgan ruled London by her wit, and
Lady Blessington reigned at Gore House by
her grace and brilliancy, while Lady Dufferin
and Mrs Norton (of that wondrous Sheridan
race) claimed and gained the world's homage by
right of wit, beauty, and genius all combined.
Mrs Jameson also, and the Brontés held their
place right sovereignly, and Mrs S. C. Hall was
a social power both in Ireland and England.
Here was a splendid band of gifted women (all
Irish by the way) who were as brilliant and
interesting in conversation as they were powerful with the pen.   Later on we find the female
intellect supremely illustrated only by the name
of one woman, Elizabeth Barrett Browning.
She stands alone without a rival in the century,
but then she stands alone amidst the women of
all centuries.   After the death of the great
poetess of England, the royal race of women
who reign by right divine of intellect disappears,
and the Professional Beauty seized the vacated
throne as a social power.   The women of genius
retreated into solitude, and are now never heard
of but on a title-page.   They no longer cast
their influence on society as brilliant thinkers
and talkers ; and a literary *salon*, ruled over by
some dazzling queen of intellect, some splendid
women of wit and learning, exists in London

no more; for, while the rush of life is tending to destroy all the forms of social etiquette, the diffusion of knowledge is sapping the foundations of the conversational art which former generations almost raised to the perfection of a science. There is nothing now left in the outer world to talk about. Penny newspapers and shilling cram satiate all curiosity, and the professional reviewers kindly crumble up for us all the current poems and novels to save society the trouble of selection or mastication. We are all fed on the same food, and have no new and strange interests to impart to each other. There are no more mysteries left. The whole world lies on our breakfast table, with all its fashions and follies, and by ten o'clock in the morning everyone knows everything that has happened throughout the universe, from the last spot on the sun to the last scandal and the latest crime. And then we glance over the society papers, where the whole thing is turned into a jest, and life is made to seem but one immense burlesque. But as conversation dies out the silent pleasures of society are gaining strength and importance. Brilliant professional genius is summoned to do all the singing, playing, talking, reciting, while society merely sits still and listens. There is music

when none dare even to whisper to his neigh-
bour a casual remark ; recitations when the room
must be hushed to perfect silence ; while at
the theatres society sits patiently, cramped and
silent, for four hours or so, and is happy that no
demand is made on it for talk. The whole
mental activity of life has become vicarious.
We lay our weariness on the head of some sub-
stitute ; and so all personal responsibility ends
for the exercise of intellect. We leave all that
to professional talent, and. except that we eat
and drink, we might as well be gods of stone,
ranged, with rigid features, round the walls of a
drawing-room, or massed in the centre like pins
in a pincushion. There is no place any more
for brilliant individuality or the small amateur
accomplishments. Trained talent has seized
the brain of the world, and grown rich on the
monopoly ; as the merchants have seized the
commerce and transmuted all they touch to gold.
Society is frozen into a mere aggregate of pas-
sive recipients and listeners, much depressed by
the consciousness of their own insignificance
and inferiority ; while the professionals receive
the plaudits and the pay, and exult, with justi-
fiable pride, in triumphs fairly won by genius,
talent and earnest study. No chance or opening
then is left to society to manifest that it has a

human soul and the gift of speech, except the
grand old national institution of a dinner party.
There at last the long-suppressed individual may
gain confidence in his own actual and separate
existence, and joyfully exclaim, *Cogito ergo sum.*
And there is no better mode of stimulating the
slumbering fires of intellectual life ; but it must
be limited in number, and organised with a due
regard to spiritual affinity. Much thought and
study are required before we place the human
individualities side by side for three mortal
hours, without the power of change of place or
the privilege of silence. All things in nature are
under the influence of attraction and repulsion.
It is the law of all that exists, and acts with as
much force on the organisms of a dinner party
as on the molecules that compose a world.
Yet we too often arrange our social atoms in a
reckless, incoherent propinquity, without the
slightest attention to this great universal law.
And what can be sadder than a three hours'
bondage to an atom with which we have no
affinity ; while our eternally-related atom is,
perhaps, placed far down at the other end of the
festive board, and a Zahara of table-cloth lies
between us. That delightful humorist, Charles
Lever, has described with pathetic fun the depression that fell on him when he found himself

at a large dinner-party, closely wedged in between two severe looking dowagers of the solid
rank that permits no trifling, and the grave per-
sistence in eating which gave no opportunity
for any light skirmish through the fairy realms
of poetry and imagination; and he knew that
his term of penal servitude must last for the
eternity of a fashionable dinner, and that there
was no hope of escape. Lady Morgan had
clearer philosophical views ; she understood perfectly the eclectic mode and the selection of the
fittest. When a celebrity arrived in Dublin
whom she was desirous of entertaining, she sent
out no formal notes of invitation, but simply
stood at her open window in Kildare Street,
just opposite to the fashionable club, watched
the passers-by, beckoned over the suitable atoms,
stepped out on the balcony, and called down
the name and the hour, and received the ready
adhesion. All was settled in a moment, and her
parties, thus selected, were the most brilliant
and successful ever known in the city, *par
excellence*, of brilliant talkers. The debit-and-
credit mode of dinner reciprocity, when people
are asked merely as a return duty, husband and
wife, father, mother and daughter, son and
mother-in-law, is fatal to the excitement and
variety of social intercourse. A clever woman

once denounced this system of every man coming to dinner with his female, two and two, as
if they were going into the Ark. Intellectual
celebrities have often very dull wives. Excellent
women, no doubt, in the domestic relation, but
no ornament or aid to society. Clever men
bring with them the gold and jewels of wit and
learning, but the homely wives are generally
weighted with lead, and might, with much advantage to everyone, be left at home.

An immense charm, however, is added to the
social circle by the presence of a brilliant, cultivated woman, with the tact and grace that can
encourage grave and learned men to speak on
the subjects they know best, and, fortunately,
the human heart has inexhaustible yearnings,
and we can still descend into the depths of the
inner life and find something of interest, unknown, untried and unreviewed, or we can soar
to the infinite in speculation on the unfathomed
mysteries of the spiritual world, and it is precisely in this direction that society is striving to
find new subjects of discussion. People are
growing weary of the flippant grotesque which
debases every high thought and fine feeling,
and are haunted by a desire for some nobler
communion of souls, and more elevating and
purer direction of thought.

E

It is then that women's influence and her special graces in refining and raising the tone of conversation are most keenly felt.

Men do not require information, but inspiration, and may find its fullest affluence in the warm glow of a woman's appreciation and her beautiful sympathy.

The sneers of jealous rivals and adverse critics often freeze to death the sensitive organisation of the artist, the poet or the writer. They pine to bask in the radiance of praise, and find the eternal sunshine only in a woman's eyes. And much knowledge is not wanted on her part. Appreciation is more in the manner than in the words. Sometimes even a single adjective, judiciously selected, is enough. She has but to lift her expressive face to the speaker and murmur—beautiful! This one word would conquer the heart of any timid sage or aspiring poet. He is understood at last, and the most seductive of all flatteries to a clever man is the sympathy that listens and comprehends.

Women live so apart from practical life that their opinion on any grave, deep subject is really worth nothing, but the sympathy of a woman is worth everything to a cause or a human heart, and has a power that never can be aroused even by the accurate logic and best ordered facts of the better-informed sex. And there is no hypocrisy in this feminine homage to a great mind or a great idea. Women delight in being led up out of their narrow sphere of thought and action into the larger life of political excitement and wider human interests, in which men work and triumph, and if they brought their garlands to the Temple of Fame they would probably crown the statue of Genius even before that of Love.

A man crowds so much into his life, he sees all, knows all, exhausts all so rapidly, that interest and impulse soon die. He is *blasé sur tout, ennuyé de tout*, but women know little of the satiety of exhausted emotion, or of the cynicism and weariness of all things to which men are prone who have drained the cup of life to the dregs.

Hence women are ever ready to be disciples and worshippers, and have the supreme faculty of giving praise freely and generously and lovingly. They look only at the head of gold, and never see the feet of clay.

Some one remarks that the sun had his cultus and worshippers till he was found out, but a true woman never finds out the shortcomings of her sun-god. She still believes in her idol and her ideal through all temptations to scepticism.

Hero-worship never dies out in the heart of a woman. She glorifies by her praise, and sends the warm tide of human life through the heart and brain of the weary worker, who had become almost a stony abstraction by solitude and thought. Rich argosies of feeling lie beneath the surface of such natures that only a woman can bring to light, wrecks of passion and ambition, and high aims unfulfilled. A woman will raise them up and make them live again. Lord Beaconsfield's estimate of women's redemptive power over a human soul almost raised her to divinity in his mind.

'No cause,' he says, 'is won, no man is great but through a woman. No man is perfect till he has learned of a woman.'

But the qualities are rare and beautiful that can make a woman not only a divine guide to a human heart, but also a splendid power in social life. A loving woman may have only love to offer, but a brilliant woman, a queen of intellect, must be able to flash lightly over every subject and illuminate them all. She must take a run through the sciences and all literature, and understand many languages, that illustrations from every source may gleam like golden threads through the warp and woof of her conversation. She must have studied the art treasures of many capitals, and number amongst her friends the leading intellects of the age; then she may take her place as a social queen, and lead in conversation, and draw the hearts of all men to her by chords of spiritual attraction.

Yet she must not converse too much. Beyond even the grace of speech there is the grace of listening and the tact of silence, even of entire self-effacement at times, which is the homage of love rather than of worship.

Lady Byron was entirely deficient in this subtle tact that can guide and soothe the wayward, turbulent and terrible temperament of genius.

'Am I in your way, Byron?' she asked one day, entering the poet's study while he was at immortal work. 'Damnably!' was the answer of the poet-husband. And she deserved it. She had no tact, no fine instincts. She ought to have known intuitively that she was in the way, and effaced herself.

Many writers have given suggestions for well-ordered conversation, but of the moderns, Emerson, Bulwer and D'Israeli are the best worth study. Aphorisms that suit both sexes equally, abound in their writings, like these,—Never prose or dogmatise; avoid laughter and the grotesque, and mimicry above all; it disturbs the facial harmony. Never condescend to amuse.

Good talk is wasted on most people, sympathy never; beware of too much energy, shun noise and glare. The Aryan in 'Lothair' would not dine where gas was burned, and hated the screams of hired singers when he wanted to talk. All agree that veiled light is indispensable to conversation, no one could be fascinating with a gas furnace over the head ; and people should study the nervous susceptibilities of their guests. Never arrive too early, it exhausts the system ; never be malicious, it is so vulgar—this is an axiom of D'Israeli's. Santa Teresa, that greatsouled woman, never would permit detraction in her presence, 'and so,' she says, 'it came to pass that where I was, the absent were never evil spoken of.' Epigram is always better than argument in conversation, and paradox is the very essence of social wit and brilliancy; the unexpected, the strange combination of opposites ; the daring subversion of some ancient platitude are all keen social weapons ; but only assured celebrity makes society pardon orginality, for people generally resent being suddenly lifted out of their old groove by the intellectual dynamite of some audacious thinker and talker, who has no respect for the laws of social routine.

Women, especially, must beware of orginality. There is always a coalition of society against it, for it is the daring self-assertion of the individual over the many, and calls down implacable revenge. Unless, therefore, with their equals, clever women should be vigilant to tone down their conversation to the regulation pattern. It is always safer to begin with common-places, they are soothing and disarm fear. Besides, women of tact can colour the common-place with a little emotional intensity, and then society says they are 'very nice,' and they even become exceedingly popular.

As for insignificant people, they should only say what they are expected to say, and never talk of themselves, their children, servants, domestic cares, or their ailments, except to the doctor, who is paid for listening, simply because society does not in the least care for the insignificant. If gossip is introduced it should be about great men, for they belong to history, but the sayings and doings of lesser people only concern the parish. Anecdotes are best avoided in society. D'Israeli hated people 'in their anecdotage,' for the constraint of listening to a long story makes the face dull and heavy. Nor should conversation be allowed to condense into dialogue at a dinner-

party, while what is called 'chaff' is fatal to
all brilliant effort, and debases every subject,
though playful humour is always charming,
kindly and pleasant, and is like a golden fringe
to the solemn draperies of conventional life;
but the vulgar grotesque, so bitterly denounced
by Ruskin, 'whose only weapon is malice, and
whose only object is to offend,' must never be
permitted, or all dignity and mutual respect
would vanish from social life.

Clever men may assert boldly and demolish
ruthlessly with half-playful dogmatism and half-
earnest faith; and they may bewilder, astonish
and instruct, but at the same time disarm the
rancour of opposition by the light grace of
the skirmish, which claims only to be a tournament, not a battle. Women, on the contrary,
do not talk for victory, but for insight. They
should not dwell on facts which are always
dull and heavy, but glide into generalisations
which are always brilliant and never very accurate, therefore suit the unfettered fancy of a
woman; while they open out wide new paths
of thought where the guidance of a clever man
is indispensable.

Intellectual women find their chief interest in high and lofty themes and speculations, and in grand and noble ideas; their

true place and home is in the infinite and the eternal.

Woman of this nature are recognised in society by a Phidian head, a majesty of Olympian repose, and a low, penetrating voice that at once attracts and enforces attention.

The chattering, pert, flippant woman, with a sharp manner, a silly laugh, and a ready mocking retort, is insufferable to a man of culture; but a coquette, though vain and versatile, may still be charming, for she has the wish to please, which is the *Grundbegriff* of woman's fascination.

Then there are other women, who, with many high mental qualities, yet seem to take a strange pleasure in making themselves disagreeable, even to the man they love, by a hard, cynical unwomanly manner, unlovely caprices, mean suspicions, harsh judgments, and disdainful return for kindness.

Cold and heartless natures; that exert their power principally to show how keenly they can torture, and who, consequently, are as irritating to sensitive organisations as a sharp-cutting east wind.

The true crown of womanhood is a loving, trusting, believing, sympathetic womanly woman. She is the angel of a man's destiny, and no time can destroy her influence, for it is based on the supreme beauty of that charm of manner which is the outward expression of the inward grace. Such women radiate light and joy, and have the secret of perpetual youth.

Society is the best teacher of manners, and the best tonic for nerves; and society should be cultivated at all times, with intervals of solitude. The intellect is a delicate-stringed instrument that rusts if not played on, and it is by the collision of mind with mind that we learn our own value, or the need of progress; what we are and what we might be. The gold is passed through the essaying fire of competition and comparison, and is brightened by the process.

It is monotony that kills, not excitement. Dull people fail in the will to live, and so they soon lose their hold on life. Excellent good women, who give up society and devote themselves exclusively to home and homely duties, grow old so soon. 'Nothing ages like domestic happiness,' Bulwer says; and Balzac affirms, clearly and coldly, that if a woman persists in giving up society, and with it all pretensions to be attractive, she ought to expiate the sin by being sent to the country for the rest of her life.

Domestic life should be made beautiful and happy, but it must be fed with many streams like Paradise, each perpetually bringing new thoughts and ideas, like golden sands. The weary man, returning from the daily professional treadmill, has an instinctive desire for brightness, softness, grace and charm after the dingy surroundings of the day; and he finds them all in the radiance of a woman's love and converse. But the converse must be nourished by constant intercourse with the best minds and the best social influences, new books, and new people, and the ever-changing phases of social progression, or it will degenerate into a wail over household cares, and a chorus of complaint rising up from the kitchen to the nursery.

And it is especially as hostess, when she reigns supreme at her own table, that a woman requires most tact, experience and varied knowledge of life and literature. Then it is her privilege to lead and guide the conversation; with swift tact to turn the course if rocks are ahead—to evade skilfully, encourage sweetly, repress gravely. And it is only a woman that can touch the curb with so light a hand that she checks without wounding. She allows no freezing ice to form and obstruct the full, free sail of thought; but by kindliness and grace stimulates to exertion all the latent mental powers that may be around her.

Then everyone looks happy; and good talk flows like wine from a golden chalice; the mutual pleasure of giving and receiving, the consciousness of heightened fascination, the triumph of success, all combine to give radiance to the countenance, intelligence to the eyes, and eloquence to the lips. Thought flashes like light from the facets of a well-cut gem; while animation and the swift changes of ever-varying expression make all faces interesting, and some beautiful. There is no heat or vehemence in discussion, for manner is a wall of defence against aggressive over self-assertion; and the presence of a high-bred woman insures decorum and refinement.

By dignity, grace and tact she claims and receives her queenly right to the homage of courteous deference and purity of conversation; and the supreme social sovereignty of woman is never more evidenced than when she touches into harmony all the diverse and conflicting elements of social intercourse. At such times, when all the rich spiritual splendours of intellect are manifested, there is no need of any adventitious aid from other sources of enjoyment.

There is talk far above singing, and the soft ripple of Ionian mirth struck from the converse of related souls is a music worthy of a symposium of the gods.

A woman, therefore, should never resign her place as a social power. She may lose the attractions of youth, but the fascination and charm of manner and conversation still remain; and her presence will always tend to keep up the dignity of social life, and the courtly traditions of a stately age.

VENUS VICTRIX.

WOMAN lies at the base of all life, whether for good or evil. From Eden to Olympus, woman is the first word written on the page of every history and of every religion, and is the illuminated initial of every man's life. The true *Venus Victrix* of creation, her influence is infinite and illimitable, and the world has bowed, and will for ever bow, before the sceptre of womanhood. Through her beauty she reigns a queen, and through her sympathy she is the mediating priestess of human destiny; and her power over man, whether through beauty or love, through purity or sin, is the crown or the torture, the glory or the perdition, of almost every human career.

'Beware of women!' exclaims a brilliant French writer; 'if they do not crown you, they will strangle you.' Yet reason can do little against the force of beauty; the first impulse, the irresistible instinct of a man's nature is the homage to physical beauty. It has a mystic power that sweeps down all before it, the strongest and wisest. A French writer says, with the eloquent extravagance of his nation and idiom, 'What can equal a woman's beauty? Nature made the planets and the stars—well enough in their way—and the flowers and the waving trees, and the red sunsets crimsoning the ocean—very praiseworthy effects all of them, and evidences of a soul endowed with fine sensibilities; but to have invented woman, with the rose-tinted white of her complexion, her hair, her lips, her eyes, her hand, the marble roundness of her arm—this was beyond the power of Nature, with all her skies and sunsets and suns and stars. To create woman required the genius of a God.'

Beauty reigns without effort, charms without trouble, fascinates without art. She simply lifts her veil, and male humanity falls at her feet. This is an unfair advantage, certainly, over the rest of the sex; but it is inevitable—a fixed decree of nature. Not with all the resources of wealth and intellect, of art and science, can less-favoured woman ever hope to achieve the triumphs which beauty obtains by a single glance.

Yet nature gives compensation and has her

revenges. Beauty may have her priesthood of poets and artists; still there are other gifts and graces by which woman can reign over hearts, and often with a more lasting power than even beauty can command.

A beautiful woman is too often vain and selfish. She seldom loves ; yet she is charming in her momentary fancies that seem like passion, but are only caprices. She is a cruel goddess, and demands victims, for her heart is stone. She worships nothing except her own lovliness. A man will die for such a woman ; but she remains calm, and drinks the spirit of his life without remorse. The whole world seems all too little for her insatiable greed of conquest and adulation. She is the sorceress, the Lamia, that fascinates and kills. She is terrible and must be propitiated, as the Egyptians hung gorgeous bracelets on the captive crocodile. Insolent when loved, implacable if slighted, her influence wraps a man round like a poisoned garment, and the fire of it consumes his life and soul.

Then it sometimes happens that, wearied and exhausted with vain idol worship, man feels the need of a redemptive force, and it is a woman's hand that draws him up to the light. It is a woman that keeps watch by the sepulchre for the uprising of a slain and buried soul ; and thus she triumphs, also a *Venus Victrix*, through the sublime and holy power of sympathy, which is a glorified form of love. She pours out the wine of life for the one beloved, and asks nothing in return from earth or heaven, only the divine joy of sacrifice, the ecstatic sense of self-annihilation for true love's sake.

This homage rendered to another—this life lavished without dream or hope of recompense—this worship given freely and disinterestedly as to a god—is the true essence of womanhood.

A strange fascination lies in this passionate sympathy; and the power which through its subtle influence a noble-hearted woman can exercise over a man's life is not by any means dependent on youth or beauty, or fashion, or dress, or even brilliant gifts. It has a moral grace higher than all these things—a diviner beauty, which is of the soul. The women gifted with this mystic charm are unfettered by chronology. They are ever young, with the eternal youth of the spiritual nature. To sensitive and clever men they are peculiarly attractive, for they seem to give them a second soul, a fuller life. They alone can intensify the aspirations of a man of genius;

F

sustain his noblest instincts; and appreciate
and comprehend his diviner nature, with that
perfect knowledge which in a woman always
travels along the line of sympathy with swift
electric vitality.

As Benjamin Constant said of Madame
de Stael when under the influence of her
marvellous powers of intellectual fascination,
'Such a woman shuts out the universe for
you.'

It is impossible almost to formulate in words
the full mystery of this highest love, which, in
its grandest manifestation, only genius gives,
and only genius can worthily appreciate. But
even less gifted natures gain from it a glory
that illuminates all life. It has no element of
the morbid selfish passion that first fevers and
then painfully wearies. The holy and beautiful
love of sympathy 'thinketh no evil.' It is the
sunshine under whose influence all the finest
impulses flourish and expand. As the Persian
poet has said, ' It is like the purple in the garment of a king, splendid in itself, and splendid
in the light it radiates.'

Women capable of this exalted feeling would
rather love than be loved, for love in its highest
meaning is aspiration, the instinct of ascension
towards the Divine. To love, therefore, is the

highest joy of the noblest soul, and lifts the
woman to the angel nature.

Still, all women, when they first open their
eyes on life, have the dream of being loved ;
and to all, perhaps, is given one moment of
supreme joy—one hour to believe that love is
eternal, but a whole life to find out that it is
an illusion. Yet, standing on the ruin of her
own dreams, as on a pedestal, woman rises to
the height of a diviner life, and can still reign
a *Venus Victrix* through the holy beauty of
sympathy and sacrifice.

It is remarkable that throughout all epochs
of history we find this feminine instinct to aid
the work of men, and intensify the spirit and
tendency of the age which he leads and dominates, symbolised by the woman in her dress.

Greek life was a glad ritual to heroes and
gods, and the Greek women in their free,
beautiful chiton, chlamys and himation, seemed
like a procession of priestesses to a temple,
or like the band at a choric festival, wreathed
and garlanded, moving to the Doric or the
Lydian measure, to celebrate the triumphs and
victories of kings and heroes.

Then came the Church which denounced
human nature as vile and sinful, and at once
the lovely form of woman was hidden under

the shrouding garments of sanctity. The long,
lovely hair was sacrificed, and in time the cord
and the cross, emblems of pain and suffering
and humiliation, replaced the glittering ornaments of youth and the radiant raiment of the
vain world's fashion. The anchorite spirit of
the Church, which drove men into the lonely
rock-caves of the desert, and taught the sublimity of renunciation, impelled beautiful women
also to desire death rather than life. They went
to martyrdom as to a bridal, and dreamed of
no other lover save the mystic Bridegroom of
the Soul.

Thus it has been ever with women, they
adopt these feminine hieroglyphs of dress to
show their union with the ideal of a man's
life, even when they are debarred from sharing
the action.

In the fierce middle ages, when society was a
camp and a battle-ground—when warrior knights,
iron-souled and iron-handed, fought and died at
the tournament for a lady's smile—then women
also became warriors in their dress, and the stiff
brocaded corslet and robe of the proud chatelaine
simulated in its rigid outline the steel-linked
cuirass of her haughty lord.

But the fierce feudal ages passed away in the
ceaseless mutation of all things, and gave place

to the dissolute splendours of the monarchies of
Europe, when luxury and pomp, tyranny and
cruelty, the mirth and madness of sin, reigned
supreme in the brilliant poisoned atmosphere
of courts, and women 'fairer than heaven, more
terrible than hell,' sat by their crowned lovers,
and drained the wine of pleasure from jewelled
cups, with their foot on the neck of the prostrate
people. It was an age of vain voluptuous
pleasure and affected mannerism, and the dress
was the expression of the life, gorgeous and
haughty, vain, luxurious and artificial. The
influence of women tended to evil alone, and
the retribution was dreadful in its vengeance.

An hour came when the people, indignant at
their degradation, threw off the bondage of
kings, princes, nobles and courtesans, and a
torrent of blood swept over the splendour and
sins of the false and fatal eighteenth century.

On its ruins arose the serene majesty of the
Republic, and the women of that era at once
strove to preach the new doctrines of liberty by
the symbolism of dress. A return to the antique
simplicity of manner and true dignity of life was
illustrated by classic drapery, sandalled feet and
hair bound with a golden frontlet, as in the days
of Socrates and Plato.

The second Empire, under the sway of a

lovely woman, restored for a time the traditions
of courtly magnificence ; but a new machinery
of civilisation had already begun to work, which,
impelled by the advance of science, is gradually
changing the whole routine of society, levelling
and destroying all the old barriers of caste, and
form and usage, with all ' the pleasant old conventions of our false humanity.' How, indeed,
could the grand and stately dignity of queenly
symbolism be any longer possible in a world
where the breathless, ceaseless, restless work of
life is carried on, even by women ?

The march of civilisation has therefore neces-
sitated the toilette of progression, and the queens
of society now demand not only political and
educational equality with man, but also identity
with the free and formless fashion of male
costume.

The model woman of the nineteenth century
inclines towards a divided skirt, a Newmarket
coat, a jockey cap ; she carries a cigarette in her
mouth, a whip at the end of her parasol, a stiletto
in her fan, and in her hand is the roll of resolu-
tions she is to enforce at the next public meeting
upon a crowd of men.

She no longer glides—the emphasis of decision
is in her very footfall, and the feverish energy
of action in the swing of her arms or the plunge

of her hands into the depths of her coat-tail
pockets.

She tramples on the old social traditions of
artificial life, and, free and fearless, upholds
health and nature above all things.

Horace Walpole maintained that it was fatal
to one's reputation to appear at breakfast, and
that no one should be fascinating before five
o'clock ; but the modern woman has organised
an 'early-rising society.' Byron declared that
no woman should be seen to eat ; but she dis-
claims this weak pretence of fragile health, and,
proud of her youth and strength, the new type
of woman (according to Mr Mallock) eats like a
sacred chicken — and we know the sacred
chickens were vigorous and voracious.

Life used to be a temple where woman was
priestess, or a court where woman was queen,
borne along in her gorgeous litter on the
shoulders of slaves. Now life is a school board,
where woman takes the chair, and adapts herself successfully to her new position and duties.

One mourns over the long hair snipped, the
flowing train abridged to a bunch or diminished
to a bow ; vain and futile endeavour to simu-
late what once had noble amplitude and royal
significance. Yet, after all, the latter-half-nine-
teenth-century women is a fine, high-spirited

creature, advanced in politics and philosophy, cultured, learned and independent, resolute in will, and fearless in her efforts to break all bondage for herself and others, as a Jael or a Judith, or a Madame Roland, who dies for liberty on the scaffold.

We must, therefore, accept the modern dress, short, hard, concise as a telegram, as best suited to the modern life of energetic work and ceaseless unrest; where there is no place for splendour, no time for variety of costume, and no room by steamer or rail for the luggage of luxury of the travelling millions who circulate round the world in endless vortices.

According to the latest decree, therefore, of the strong-minded, all that is now required by a lady if she takes a Cook's ticket to Jericho and the Pyramids, is a costume of black calico and an umbrella.

The age of splendour has passed, and a dreadful uniformity of homeliness and utility pervades all classes. Everyone seems turned out by machinery, and no one has leisure to study the individual requirements of face and figure; the symphonies of colour, the cadence of lines, the rhythm of accord and contrast, with all the subtle harmonies that make perfect dress like a full chord of music.

Women aim now only at being intelligent and intellectual, and the toilette of work has replaced the charming fascination of luxury and idleness.

So in our modern world we seek in vain for living representatives of the stately formality of Holbein, the regal grace of Sir Peter Lely, the high-bred courtly coquette of Gainsborough's era, or the exquisite elegance of Sir Joshua Reynolds. These types have gone for ever. The realism of ulsters and newmarkets, the democracy of dress, is making all our social life colourless and unpicturesque; consequently this age will not, perhaps, add any immortal female portraits to the picture galleries of England.

M. Taine complains of the cold callousness of English women to beautiful effects in dress. Their clothes, he says, seem fitted as if on a wooden frame, without art, without visible intention ; whereas the object should be to enhance beauty where it exists, or to create it if necessary by the laws of art.

Variety, above all, is attractive ; if possible, a woman should never appear twice in the same dress, except, of course, at lectures on primary molecules or the revolution of atoms, or the Unknowable, and subjects of that grave and

awful kind ; for professors and philosophers
and learned men generally never know what
a woman wears. But poets and artists, and
others of sensitive human organisation require
the charm of varying light and colour.

Humanity is distinguished from the ape by
two things — laughter and dress. Women,
therefore, should assert their humanity by
triumphs in dress, to prove their advanced
position in the scale of beings.

Besides, dress charms at all ages. The
beauty of form and feature passes away ; the
coquette dies with youth ; even accomplishments weary ; but style lasts for life, and
never fails to please. It confers a patent of
nobility on a woman, and gives her a distinguished and eminent status in social circles.

Yet, woman seem growing careless as to
this great source of female power, with all its
mystic and subtle fascinations, and the stage
is now the only exponent of beauty of design
in form and colour.

Lady Martin—Helen Faucit—was the first
to raise theatrical costume to the dignity of
artistic expression by the perfect grace in fall
and flow of lines and draperies ; not by the
endeavour to pile up fabrics remarkable only
for reckless cost, but by producing pictures in

form and colour such as painters and sculptors love to contemplate.

Helen Faucit, however, had the brow of a Greek muse, and a form lithe and undulating as the graceful figures on a Greek vase ; and thus was able to realise effectively her own ideal of classic grace and beauty.

Recently, also some admirable and picturesque effects in theatrical costume were produced from designs by Mr Godwin, the architect, and Lewis Wingfield, artist and novelist, which harmonised admirably with the delicate, ethereal, wayward grace of Madame Modjeska, and the superb dramatic beauty of Genevieve Ward, while the charming Grace Hawthorne, always perfectly illustrates the dramatic idea, by the artistic accuracy of her beautiful costumes.

At the Lyceum, under Mr Irving's management, one is always certain of a series of perfect pictures, the result of deep artistic study and profound knowledge of pictorial and scenic effect. And in Mr Gilbert's bright operetta of ' Patience ' the piece, though meant to satirise the cultus of beauty, actually gained proselytes to the æsthetic movement, so infinitely charming were the ' love-sick maidens in their Greek dresses of flowing lines and beautiful combination of colour, while the modern style which they afterwards assume is quite repellent to the nerves from its rude and crude angularity and rigid outline.

Without this pictorial teaching, now brought to such perfection on the stage, one might almost forget the power of tones and form and colour to enhance female beauty ; for an ordinary crowd in the daily life of this great Babylon of London seems but a heavy mass of opaque obscurity thrown upon the background of a sunless sky, blackness above, around, and beneath. Can we wonder, then, if depression or ill-temper is the result ? for nothing generates a morbid discontent like sombre, monotonous, ineffective costume, without any illuminating point of colour to break the uniformity of that national gloom of dress which in England is considered for a woman the *vrai cachet du comme il faut.*

Uniformity of style is also equally depressing, when all women look as if they were cut after the same paper pattern, and all interesting attractive distinctions of individuality are destroyed.

A woman, on the contrary, should first study her own personality, and consider well what she means to be, desires to be, and can be—either a superb Juno, or a seductive Aphrodite, or a Hebe, blooming and coquette, or a Pallas Athene, grand, majestic and awe-inspiring. And, when the style is discovered that bests suits her—it may be for homage or for love—let her keep to it as the symbol of her higher self, unchanged by the frivolous mutations of fashion. For dress thus attains a moral significance, and becomes the exoteric expression of the esoteric spiritual nature.

Now, for the first time in the history of the world, a path is opening to female intellect, energy and talent, and, henceforth, women, perhaps, may lead in the learned professions, take their part in home government, form ministries to organise the code of female rights, and claim the highest university honours, in rivalry with men. Will they be happier? Will it be lost in the coming time, the grace of indolent luxury, the supreme fascination of beauty, when the career of severe study and training begins in earnest, if women are to compete successfully with men in the great chariot race of progress in the arena of life? Who can say? A wider sphere of action and higher aims certainly will make their life nobler, and therefore, perhaps, happier.

Woman may gain even truer claims to ad-

miration through the life of work which gives
her dignity and honour, than she has yet attained
by all her petty accomplishments, the feeble
efforts of a prisoned intellect.

The race of the gifted—the artists and poets
and thinkers—have rarely a definite law of life :
they are simply masses of emotional force, alter-
nations of violent impulses and silent despair.
Their genius is a lava stream, that often devas-
tates the life, though it may turn the rudest
stones to gems, as it rushes onward. It is a
woman's mission to guide, control, direct and
calm these storms of passionate emotion, and
she will better comprehend the mystic and wayward nature of the intellectual temperament
through her own experience of its trials and
claims.

Manners even may become nobler because not
so artificial, and the earnestness of thought and
feeling will replace the mere coquetry of vanity
and display. It is only shallow natures, accord-
to D'Israeli, that mistake noise for gaiety and
persiflage for wit. Dress also will be more
beautiful because simpler and freer from the
tortuous elaborations for which earnestness and
intellect have no time or inclination.

The woman of the future will never again
be the mere idol of a vain worship, the petted

toy of a passing hour. She takes her place now in the world on higher grounds than physical beauty, and will gain nobler triumphs; for it is impossible to believe that woman will be less attractive because educated, less tender and devoted because learned, less loving because she can attain the high station, honour, dignity and wealth, which hitherto only marriage could confer, by her own unfettered intellect and genius.

But, through all modes and moods of changing life, the woman's heart will still reign paramount over the woman's brain. In the ceaseless strife against ignorance and sin and fate, woman will ever be on the side of mercy, helping the weak, the wronged, the suffering, and giving light to darkened lives — the true angel of humanity; while the power she gains from intellect and knowledge will but give her a stronger redemptive force, a sublimer zeal in the cause of right and truth.

All that is noblest and most beautiful in a woman's nature is eternal. No time changes, no trials weaken, no ingratitude even chills, the warm impulse of a woman's heart. Priestess and paraclete she will ever be, as she has ever been ; and now, as a queen also, in the new and wider sphere of intellectual power and social dignity, she will stand beside man, his equal and co-worker, giving her aid to the great cause of light and freedom, with all that uplifts human souls from ignorance and degradation ; but claiming still her proud title of *Venus Victrix* through the divine grace and sacred mystery of sympathy, that holiest sacrament of life, which binds the destiny of woman to man.

Thus, a nobler humanity will be the revelation of the coming age, brought to a more splendid perfectness by woman's influence in that divine life of love and work and intellect, which finds men human, but which leaves them gods.

SPIRITUAL AFFINITY.

WILLIAM VON HUMBOLDT, brother of the great Alexander, and eminent himself as a profound and scientific philologist, seems to have been one of the few men to whom it was given to realise the charm of a true, tender and spiritual affection existing between man and woman, quite apart from all physical attraction, if only their souls were eternally related. His thoughts on the subject, expressed with all the lofty serenity of the philosophic temperament, may be studied with interest in his volume, entitled *Letters to a Lady*.

Humboldt and the lady to whom they are addressed met only for a few days' intercourse, when both were young. Many years passed, and they held no communication, yet a mutual and ineffaceable impression had been made, and a spiritual relationship was established, entirely unlit by any glow of human sensuous love.

Then a correspondence began that lasted over ten years, during which time they seem never to have met.

G

Humboldt's letters during this time betray much of the calmness of spirit which is the highest ideal of pagan philosophy. To him this calmness, perhaps, was natural, for he describes himself as all his life singularly free from the fever of the passions. Many of his aphorisms might pass for extracts from the manual of Epictetus, they are so similar in spirit. He seems almost insensible to pain, error, and all the changes and chances of this mortal life, yet he has no harsh or uncongenial nature, no 'Manfred misanthropy,' having 'no sympathies with breathing flesh,' for he says in one letter,—'One can never hear or see enough of one's own species: every new aspect in which we behold it is fruitful of ideas. In every man, however insignificant, there is hidden a noble and thoughtful nature, which is the more noble as he is the more virtuous.' But here is Epictetus and his serene philosophy,—'My endeavours have ever been directed to two objects—one, to attain a perfect knowledge of every phase of life—the other, to be dependent on no one, not even on Fortune herself, but to stand firmly on my own vantage ground, and to rely on my own resources. I am happy beyond other men, because few men have so few wants. The satisfying of a want is but the stilling of a pain,

and is opposed to all pure, reposeful enjoyment.'
Again,—'I never fear misfortune, even when it
stands upon my threshold; I look on it as an
uncheerful, but by no means as an evil companion.' Nor can outward affairs disturb the
serenity of his mind; he lives in the essentials,
not dependent on the incidents of life,—'To
exchange,' he says, 'for instance, the most
agreeable for the most disagreeable abode,
would be to me a matter of perfect indifference.
I have no wants, except the chair on which I
sit, and the table at which I write. Any room
is the same to me, and in mine are no luxuries,
no mirrors, no sofa.' Speaking of past griefs,
he considers the retrospect no evil, 'for it ever
possesses for me a certain kind of sweetness, and
I love it, moreover, for the assistance which it
gives me in gaining that independence of fortune
so indispensable to a manly character.'

Nor can the weather even relax the strings of
his soul. 'Be it foul or fair,' he says, 'I receive
it with as much indifference as the smiling or
terrible scenes in a theatre.' Nor can praise
strengthen their tension,—'Praise is not worth
much, and I always receive it as metal which
has not been assayed, and which, if I do not use
caution, may probably be a source of injury.'
Pain is treated as no evil. He cannot even

prevail on himself to call illness one, and the
philosopher, suffering from a severe cold and
toothache, thus speaks,—'When sickness approaches me, it ever comes attended with a
species of rest and serenity to the soul; not
that I am without those qualities in good health,
but that in health man is kept in an atmosphere
of zeal and energy which falls away in time of
sickness.' The loss of youth, too, has its charms
for him. This fleeting away of our *Lebens
goldne zeit,* over which Schiller mourns so
exquisitely, sheds no gloom on his spirit. He
says,—

' I always looked forward to old age with peculiar delight, and now that I am approaching it, I
find my expectations surpassed. The greatest
gain which springs from it is spiritual freedom—
freedom from passion. The disposition is serene
and time-softened ; the reflection purer, stronger,
better sustained ; the intellectual horizon clearer,
and the soul, occupying itself with every kind of
knowledge, and every kind of truth, has no other
desire. A contemplative, enquiring life is the
highest state of existence in the world, and can
only be enjoyed perfectly in age. Life is a vast
immense of waters, through whose contending
currents we must guide our trembling bark, and
it is most natural to rejoice when a large portion

of the journey is accomplished. The things of
the world have no longer any interest for me'—
he was then fifty-seven—'but pass by me as
momentary visions, with which neither my mind
nor my spirit has any connection. The circle of
my acquaintance narrows every day ; my dearest
friends are dead, but contemplation is an im-
measurable field of knowledge and discovery,
which ever offers new charms. I have often
passed whole days entirely occupied with my
own thoughts. It is an important consideration
that men crowded closely together become
selfish. We must retreat from the crowd of
humanity to the heights of nature; by such
means alone can a man leave the world of sense
and live in the universe of thought. The fear
of death is diminished; we learn to look on it
but as a mere transformation, as one of the
natural consequences of the design of our
being. Old age is, in reality, but as youth,
an entrance into life ; an exaltation of the
thoughts.'

Darley, the dramatist, has expressed something of the same idea in one of his plays,—
' Youth is sadder than age in its decline, for it is
falling to a *lower* state of existence, but age is
rising to a *higher.*' Humboldt has the highest
appreciation of the silent beauty of a woman's

life, and of that light, like still sunshine, which
women cast from their own peculiar sphere of
influence upon the stormy waters of man's more
troubled existence. ' I love,' he says, ' above all
things, the laboriousness of women, and the
labours to which they attach themselves permit
them, peculiarly, to live a life of feeling and
ideas. To this I attribute the deep, beautiful,
earnest disposition which most women enjoy so
beyond that of men who have even received a
higher education.' Dwelling in greater seclusion,
their souls hold more frequent and earnest communion with themselves, and the very solitude
to which social laws banish her he thinks of
'great value to a woman, elevating her soul, so
tender and earnest in itself, purifying and with-
drawing it from all those little, mean and dis-
tracting pursuits into which women fall so much
more easily than men. There are women, also,
who love solitude instinctively and naturally,
and are drawn to it by the higher aid it gives to
the exalted moods of the soul. But they are
exceptional natures, the women of genius, who
realise the idea that joy comes not from outer
things, but from the depths of their own inner
being. And the love given to such women by
a man, who can appreciate high qualities, is
unchangeable, and knows no diminution from

the passing years, or the fading tints of youthful beauty.

In every position, Humboldt maintains, woman's life is insulated, therefore more spiritual than that of man, and to draw her into the fierce arena and battle-ground of life, would blight and ruin all that is most beautiful and elevated in her nature. For woman is not made for combat or self-assertion, but for sympathy and self-sacrifice, and she can only reach to the higher plane by the annihilation of self. Thus, the inner spiritual life is developed more truthfully and purely in woman than in man, for men grow hard and selfish and crabbed by the dull routine necessity of work laid on them, where the toil is not lightened by love. While toil, no matter how arduous, is borne cheerfully by a wife or mother for the sake of those she loves, and often without any recompense.

Speaking of his own age to his fair, but no longer youthful, friend, he says,—'This reminds me that I do not know your exact age, and I consider it of great importance to know the ages of my friends, especially of such as are females. I have my own thoughts on women's ages, and prefer those somewhat advanced in years to

those who are younger.' He, at least, did not
hold to the dogma that—

> ' There flows through all the dells of Time
> No stream like youth again.'

for in his opinion 'women's personal charms
continue to unfold to a much later period than
is generally supposed, and that their minds are
much improved by years is manifest. I have
never cared,' he says, 'to form a friendship with
a woman much younger than myself, and certainly would not have married one. Similarity
in all conditions of the soul is necessary for
exalted intercourse, and a man can only find
great joy in marriage when his wife agrees,
according to the different nature of her intellect,'
with all the thought and feeling of his soul.
His notions on friendship are peculiarly just and
true. It must be free, trusting and spontaneous,
demanding nothing, needing nothing, for that
would be but an interchange of compassion,
which is, 'a distressful feeling,' or of sympathy,
which is very beautiful, but only so to a certain
extent.

The condition of a perfect friendship is, that
each should be sufficient of himself for himself.
A joyous, sunny, blissful feeling of spontaneous
admiration, each walking in his own light, yet

rejoicing in the glory of the mingled radiance.
Nor is friendship to come too near, with its
microscope examining the small motives that,
mayhap, may guide our greatest actions, nor
with its smoked glass discovering the spots that
may sometimes dim their lustre. A sacred
reserve is as necessary to friendship as to love.
'Even to my wife,' he says, 'I do not impart
my joys and sorrows, nor the accidents of life
that jostle me about; there are nobler subjects
of discourse. Friendship and love demand the
most entire confidence, and with *inquisitive souls*
there is no confidence.' How true is that!
Friendship (particularly between two beings of
opposite sexes) he calls 'a wonderful relation.'
'They share in common that Inner Life of the
soul, wherein each yields up their own peculiar
existence to the other, yet preserves it in a state
of greater clearness and purity by the contact.'
Deux âmes qui se touchent sans se confondre, as
a Frenchman has defined the 'wonderful relation.' Love has a sensuous element in it, and
there is earthliness in all passion, it is common
to all natures, the lowest as the highest; but the
feeling of friendship is the peculiar prerogative
of only the highest, tenderest and most gifted
souls. Speaking of spring, he says, and many
minds will echo the thought,—'Your sorrowful

emotions at this, the period of Nature's resurrection, are common to all who think deeply
and carefully, without, by any means, injuring
the pleasure with which they greet her after her
long sleep. The sadness of these emotions is
the result of their earnestness, for all the earnest
emotions of humanity are sad. The instability
of all life is never so manifest to us as at the
change of the seasons ; the sight of the joyous
life of the world of leaves and flowers, so free
from any trace of winter, is as deeply moving
as the sight of a child who knows not care,
whom care knows not.' All poets have found
the strings of their harp to sound more mourn-
fully when touched by the spring winds. How
beautifully, says the Italian lyrist, comparing
the glowing, hopeful life of beauty in the
external world around, with the desolate winter
reigning, perhaps, in the soul that contemplates
it,—

> ‘ O primavera, gioventu de l'anno,
>   Tu torni ben, tu torni,
>   Ma teco altro non torni
>   Che la rimembranza misera, e dolente.
>   Tu quella se, tu quella,
>   Ch' eri pur dianzi si vezzosa e bella,
>   Ma non son io gia quel ch'un tempo fui ! ’

And the great Spaniard Cervantes not less
pathetically exclaims,—‘ La primavera sigue al

verano, el verano al estio, sola la vida humana
corre al su fin, sin esperar renovarse sino es en
la otra vida.'

Yet saddest of all is that tearful line where
Schiller says of the brief spring of his own
suffering existence :—

'Doch Thränen gab der kurze Lenz mir nur.'

So the correspondence between Humboldt
and the lady went on for years, and their friendship remained unchilled, for influences that
touch the soul are eternal, and spiritual affinity
is a deathless passion, unlike the more transient
delirium of the senses. It rests ever calmly on
the serene heights of the psychical life, and is
never touched or tortured by the exactions of
jealousy, or the irritation of waning temper ;
and not even the sad evidences of fading youth
and beauty can mar or kill the affection which
is based, not upon sensuous and, therefore, evanescent attraction, but on the eternal harmony
of related souls.

SUITABILITY OF DRESS.

NOTHING, in general, bewilders or tortures the
female mind more than the endeavour to
establish some kind of harmonic relation between the law of the fashion book and the
law of life, the one being for the idler, the
other for the worker. Yet with some resolute
self-assertion and heroic defiance of conventional prejudice, a compromise might be
effected, the result being increased comfort to
the workers in life's thorny paths without
even the sacrifice of beauty. Rather would a
fresh beauty be added to woman by the fitness and propriety of costume, always so
pleasant to the wearer, and so agreeable to
the eye of the artistic spectator.

The Roman Catholic Church, that so well
understands the working of the innermost
wheels of our complex human nature, at once
recognised the truth that dress and vocation
should be in harmony, and that besides being

a symbol, dress should be a help. Hence the soft, simple, shrouding robes of the holy sisterhoods, where nothing is permitted of showy material or marked delineation of form to jar upon penitent humility, or to irritate the sad and sick, the weary-hearted or world-worn but everything in the costume is grave, calm and noiseless, to soothe and lull like low music. Loud dressing, the glare of colour, the rustle of starch, the *frou-frou* of silk, are all such cruel discords, when mind and body are lying faint and weak and low, while the soft woollen robes that glide and float with soundless motion are entirely sympathetic and soothing.

Even Protestantism—stern, cold and logical —is beginning to find out the value of those subtle influences that act on the nerves, and excite or calm emotion through other agents than logic and reason, so the Protestant sisterhoods have adopted almost universally the robes suitable to works of mercy and charity, of soothing and healing. All the reckless experiments of vanity are being replaced by the grace and harmony that lie in fitness and suitability.

In another large class of workers the study of dress as influencing nerve power is of vast importance. It has been computed that about sixteen thousand women in London live by literature, that is, there are amongst us sixteen thousand bundles of abnormal nerves and sensibilities and quivering emotions, fiery fancies, tumultuous passions, and throbbing brains, all working day and night to formulate themselves into words. Now, it is well known that to aid the process of composition, all literary people require a peculiar diet — light, cool and simple — so do they require a peculiar style of dress—cool and simple also.

Fashion is an idol they can never worship. To them whatever impedes the continuity of thought is suicidal. While weaving garments for the children of their brain, they must fling aside all care for the garments of the body. Time is to them a golden sand that cannot be wasted, and the process of an elaborate toilette might utterly efface from the mind all the thick-coming fancies that must be caught flying, or they will come no more.

For this reason Georges Sand, the great French authoress, never wore but one style of dress, a black silk. She said that she could neither waste her time on fashion, nor her temper on rivalry, with other women in the matter of dress, so when she accepted invitations to large assemblies, she stipulated for a separate boudoir where she could receive a select circle of brilliant thinkers and friends without the necessity of clothing herself in any unusual paraphernalia.

The literary dress should, in fact, be free, untrammelled and unswathed. As simple and as easily adjusted as Greek drapery, and fastened only with a girdle or a brooch. No stiff corselet should depress the full impulses of a passionate heart. There should be no false coils upon the head to weigh upon the brain, no fuzzy furze bush on the brow to heat the temples and mar the cool logic of some grand, deep thought. And the fewer frills, cuffs and cascades of lace the better, for ink-spots do not improve Venetian point, and in moments of divine fury or feverish excitement the authoress is often prone to overturn her ink-bottle.

Nothing to mind, nothing to care about, no bondage through fashion or vanity either on soul or body should be the law of dress for literary women.

The comfort of an easy, well-known garment to the literary worker is amusingly

illustrated by Diderot in one of his letters.
A grand new scarlet dressing-gown had been
given to him, but bitterly he laments the
loss of the old one it replaced.

'What induced me to part with it?' he
exclaims. 'It was made for me, and I for
it. It moulded itself to all the turns of my
body without fretting me. It was picturesque
and beautiful. There was no want to which
its complaisance did not lend itself, for indi-
gence is very obsequious. Were a book
covered with dust, one of the lappets was
ready to wipe the dust away. If the ink refused to flow freely from my pen, it proffered
a fold. You saw traced on it in long black
lines the man of letters, the writer, the worker,
and now—I only look like a rich idler. I
was the absolute master of my old robe. I
am now the slave of my new one. Care
wraps me about. I do not weep or sigh,
but I say, cursed be the costly robe that I
stand in awe of. Alas! Where is my old,
my humble, my obliging piece of homespun?'
and so on, with much humour but real truth,
he laments in a right pleasant way the
bondage of fine clothes that kills thought
and tames the spirit. Freedom from all
petty social observances and fashions is also

one of the chief instincts of all mental workers, hence the tendency amongst male writers to long hair and loose necktie; and certainly no inspiration could have come to the Pythia had she worn a corselet and hoop.

But it is comparatively easy to theorise on the fitting dress for saints or authors; their line of life and work is so distinctly marked. It is not so easy to lay down a law suitable to ordinary daily life. Wives and mothers will always find it difficult to dress suitably for visits of inspection to the nursery and the kitchen, and at the same time elegantly enough to receive chance visitors in the drawing-room.

Balzac had the worst opinion of a woman who came down to him from the nursery fashion-finished, with cost and care. It gave him the idea that she was vain and heartless, and not attending to her duties. He would have preferred hair tossed by baby fingers, dress crumpled by baby caresses.

As a rule, for the domestic employments, something light and inexpensive, yet bright and gay, should be selected; if easily spoiled as easily replaced. Something to poetise by colour and glow the prosaic monotony and ugliness of daily cares. And as to visitors, they must be left to a fixed reception day. No lady who has

H

any regard for time or study or employment should permit the disintegration of her day by casual visitors, who come in, probably, because they were passing, or because they were too early for the train, or because, in fact, they were idle and idling, and had no remorse in wasting moments very precious to thinkers and doers.

For afternoon receptions black should be sedulously avoided, either for the receiving or received. Black is unlovely and unbecoming to everyone, especially to English women, with the delicate half tints of their colouring, and the murky grey of the atmosphere. Besides it absorbs the light and spoils the effect of rooms, making it difficult to light them. Nothing can be more dreary at afternoon teas than rows of opaque, black bundles along the walls of a drawing-room, like masses of hummocky ice, particularly when black bonnets and black veils are added. White bonnets and white veils, on the contrary, are bright and pleasant, and give a soft cloud-like atmosphere to the rooms by which all faces are beautified, and whatever colouring may be in eyes, lips, cheek, and hair is heightened and intensified.

Englishwomen seem to have a fatal predisposition towards black, and having reached the middle term, the *mezzo-cammin'* of life, generally

retire into a black alpaca for the remainder of
their days. This voluntary adoption of the
symbol of doom is very sad; they ought to
remember that variety of dress and the refresh-
ing brightness of colour is charming at all ages,
and fills house and home with a flush of gladness and joy which almost replaces the loss of
youth. One of the great beauties of the Court
of Louis Quatorze, as she grew old, adopted all
the delicate shades of colour for her dress, but
never black. Age, she said, was sombre enough;
why make it more so by dress? And, coquette
to the last, she gave loveliness even to the
shadows of advancing years by the exquisite
pale greys and lilacs of her costume that
changed darkness to light and made every
room more beautiful in which she moved. Perhaps the influence of Her Majesty has led to
this general adoption of black in London as the
national dress. For the Queen has never been
seen by her subjects since her widowhood but
as a mass of black; dress, bonnet, gloves, parasol, all shrouded in the same deep and mysterious
gloom. The Queen is probably too intellectual
to pay much attention to dress, else she would
have effected many desirable changes in her
long reign, and abolished many absurd Court
usages. For instance, could anything be more

dreadful than the custom of low dresses and
bare arms at a day drawing-room in the chill
air of a freezing February or in the remorseless
glare of a noonday sun ? Yet, Court etiquette
cannot be broken even for delicate girls or
asthmatic dowagers. The Chinese Ambassador,
commenting on this in his published journal,
expresses surprise at seeing Court ladies almost
nude, yet adds that they did not seem to mind
it, even when talking to persons of the opposite
sex.

The love of external embellishment seems
the most universal characteristic of humanity,
and should not be discouraged. The South
American Indians, with their delicate features
and magnificent hair, sweeping the ground like
a shadow when one faces the sun ; the rude
hunters of the Prairies ; the graceful Poly-
nesians, with their soft, beautiful eyes, superb
hair, and elegant forms, pliant as their own
fern palms ; the wild Californian, with the long
plugs of wood, tipped with feathers, exuding
from his ears and nose ; or the African prin-
cess, in her severely natural costume, consisting
of a girdle of wampum, ornaments, fishbones
—all alike are under the influence of this master
passion ; and out of paint, feathers, beads, mat-
ting tattooing, shells and brass buttons, vanity

contrives to build up the primary strata of all human emotions. Russian genius has even proved that, with an instinct of adaptation, all things may be turned to beautifiers, as all discords to harmony, by a skilful hand. Every one knows Kohl's story of the girl of St Petersburg, who was dressed up by her mother for the Bride's Fair on Easter Monday, with a row of tablespoons set round her girdle, a necklace of teaspoons and a couple of fish-trowels placed crosswise on her back.

Neither did the Greek women, with all their intellect, nor the Romans, with all their heroism, neglect the fine arts of the toilet. Jewels, gorgeous robes and costly perfumes helped 'the poisoning of the dart, too apt before to kill.' The Greeks painted their eyes like the Easterns, and stained the fingers rose colour and the lips vermilion. The Roman dress resembled the Oriental, flowing robes of silk and jewels of enormous value ; a *Toga*, or ample robe, clasped on the shoulders, and falling in rich folds to the ground; and a stola, a robe, with a long train appended to a bodice made to fit the figure ; probably the rudiment of our truly anæsthetic modern costume, which violates every principle of artistic beauty in the formation of the figure, and annihilates, as far as possible, all the grace-

ful folds and curves which drapery naturally
assumes. Veils were not as indispensable as in
the East, but some enhanced their beauty with
a shading of rose-coloured gauze, and both men
and women of the higher ranks powdered their
hair with gold dust ; but this only in the days
of the empire, and when Rome was falling, conquered by luxury. Grecian women wore a flowing robe without sleeves, girdled at the waist,
the hair braided, and sometimes crowned with
flowers and sandals on the feet. Art had
only to imitate — it could not improve this
costume, where grace, beauty and harmony
were made visible to the eye.

A history of dress would be a history of
minds; for dress expresses a moral idea; it
symbolises the intellect and disposition of a
nation. The Saxon women, in their bodice
and short petticoat, with a mantle thrown over
the head and shoulders, expressed admirably
the stern, useful, homely virtues of their race.
The Normans introduced corsets, and the high
tight bodice like a corslet, embroidered with
the family arms on each side, while a veil
floated from beneath a coronet to the feet, suit-
ing well with their proud, haughty, formal,
brocaded manners. Between the Tudor and
Stuart era, dress, like the literature of the time,

was a ponderous but gorgeous composite ; the
Puritans, however, restored it to a simplicity of
which Quakerism still remains the symbol.   The
analogy between the dress and morals of the
Restoration is too evident to need comment :
while in the high heels, wigs and whalebone of
Queen Anne's reign we find the truest exponent of the stilted, false, stiff, artificialised
mind and literature of the day.   Flour for the
hair was introduced by the Hanoverian Georges ;
for, having little in their heads, they probably
thought it the more necessary to put something
on them.

The great French Revolution restored dress
to the Republican simplicity of the tunic, sandals, and braided hair ; and now when minds
and states are trembling with vibrations that
foreshadow a speedy breaking up of all old,
outworn modes of life and thought, dress will,
no doubt, become the symbol of the higher
cultivation and increased graces of the spirit.
For women, as a rule, are always trying to show
their sympathy with the movement and tendencies of the age, by the symbolism of dress,
since they are prohibited from taking any part
in the actual work of life.

Besides, personal adornment is the natural
language of female humanity, and by it she

evinces her desire to charm, which is the strongest instinct of woman's nature.

The adornment of the head, especially, has always been a matter of much importance amongst the nations, the principal aim and object being to give dignity to the figure by increasing the apparent height. The circlet of feathers worn by the savage chief, and the golden crown of the mighty monarchs of the world were adopted to produce this effect, and thus became symbols of sovereignty and power, and inspired awe and reverence, whereas a low, flat head is expressive only of submission and servitude.

A French writer on dress observes, with reference to this subject, that a parting down the middle of the head destroys in a great degree nobility of expression, for it effaces the line of the moral arch, and thus gives the low, depressed outline, so suggestive of the head of the criminal classes.

The long train, also, was invented to give dignity to the figure by simulated height, and was at once adopted by all the royal races for their court ceremonials, as it expresses with superb grace the insolent pride of rank and caste, that would keep all lower humanity at a respectful distance.

But all these distinctive symbols that separate the classes and the masses, will soon be extinguished and crushed out by the pressure of the crowd, and the ever-increasing claims of social duties upon our time and the very small span of life we have at our command.

A century ago visiting was a stately social function. A lady of quality had her own sedan chair, kept in the hall of her spacious mansion, and in this, gorgeously attired, she was carried on her round of visits by her own bearers, while a tall footman, with uplifted stick, walked beside, to aid my lady's exits and entrances. It was a charming era of graceful idleness and pleasure for a woman, and her life was summarised thus :—

> Elle s'habille,
> Elle babille,
> Elle se déshabille.

But now the visiting list has increased from hundreds to thousands, and includes all America as well as Europe ; and there are 85,000 streets in London to traverse, which, if extended in a straight line, as has been calculated, would exceed the diameter of the earth, while overhead fifty tons of soot suspended in the atmosphere materially interferes with all attempts at gorgeous and beautiful apparel. Besides, woman has now a mission, and prefers the platform to the isolation of the sedan chair, and is rapidly taking her place as a leader in action, an inspirer of new thought, and a power and victor in the war of life. Her aims are to reform the laws, to emancipate her sex and revolutionise society; and with admirable and fluent eloquence she demands the rights due to woman, and denounces the wrongs done by man. But the new modes of thought and action, now advocated by the advanced section of existing womanhood, will gradually, no doubt, generate new habits of social usage. There will be more ease and freedom in mutual intercourse, and less bondage to routine and custom.

Everything will tend to simplify manners and conventional forms, and the life of civilisation may then, after all, become worth living, a true exponent of social comfort, and, at the same time, of high mental enjoyment.

AMERICAN WOMEN.

THE first question propounded to a traveller on returning from a transatlantic tour is usually, 'What is your opinion of American women?' for, in truth, the American woman is by far the most important element in the social machinery of the States.

Her reputation for beauty and smartness has spread over the whole earth, and to doubt her fascination would be a heresy even beyond this agnostic age. However, we are, fortunately, not wholly dependent on the crude judgment of awe-struck, startled travellers, saturated as they are with old-world prejudice, and prisoned in its narrow, conventional traditions; for the Americans, having already interviewed and exhausted all Europe, are now laudably engaged in the process of interviewing each other, and that with an acuteness and insight far beyond the observing faculty of the bewildered foreigner.

Nothing, in fact, can be more interesting than

the analytical descriptions of their own people
to be found in the pages of the great living
novelists of America; and we may certainly
accept in perfect faith the clever, clearly out-
lined sketches of eminent writers, such as
Howells, Henry James, Cable, Aldrich, Edgar
Fawcett, and other leaders of the great modern
school of fiction, as the fullest expression of
that wonderful product of social progress and
advanced intelligence—the nineteenth-century
American woman.

Every type is reproduced in their gallery of
contemporary portraits—from the fragile, luxurious beauty of the South, to the audacious
energetic newspaper woman of the North, who
scampers through Europe, note-book in hand,
interviewing everyone that has a name, and
exhausting every subject, after half-an-hour's
study, in letters of pungent criticism for her
weekly paper, dated generally from 'the express train,' 'the tunnel,' or 'the steamboat.'

Every city also has its peculiar characteristics,
and with these we are made fully acquainted
through the novelists. In Boston, for instance,
the women are 'intense' and transcendental;
it is the city of advanced intellects and the
emancipated woman. The celebrated Margaret
Fuller, the 'Zenobia' of Hawthorn's *Blithedale*

Romance, gave the first impulse there to psychical progress when she inaugurated the literary *salon* at her own house, selected and announced the subject for the evening's discussion, and brilliantly led the conversation herself. Since then Boston is the accepted exponent of the higher culture ; and the intellectual women who gather there under the shadow of the world-soul, treat life with a lofty and serene philosophy, proudly disdaining the fashion, follies and dress of New York.

Philadelphia is the Quaker city—neat, orderly, calm and reserved, where everyone seems to go to bed at ten o'clock, and the ladies make no effort to heighten the charm of their pretty faces by the adventitious aid of rouge or pearl powder. But they cultivate literature, poetry and art ; and society is elegant and refined. Among the celebrities of 'the flowery city' may be named the late Professor Gross, eminent in medical science, George Boker, one of the leading poets of America, and Mrs Bloomfield Moore, who has earned the gratitude of the citizens by her splendid donations of paintings and artistic works, valued at more than five thousand pounds, to the new Museum of Art established there.

Washington is grand and courtly ; a stately

city of rank and solemnity. The royal ambassadors set the mode, especially the English embassy, which takes the lead in style and splendour that republicans weakly try to emulate by a display of liveried servants and heraldic emblazonments. Caste and class strive eagerly there for precedence, and every young lady looks forward, confidently, to being elected to the English peerage. In that clever novel, *Democracy*, there are capital sketches of life at Washington, where the officials claim to be ultra aristocrats, and Miss Virginia Dare resolves to become a countess, in which, of course, she succeeds, for what simple English peer could resist her all-compelling energy and smartness ; in fact, the American girl is beginning to look on the English peerage as the appanage of her race. Not that she is over-elated at the prospect, for an American woman thinks nothing too good for her that can be had for love or money, no social position too eminent for her merits. If a crowned prince asked her in marriage she would consider it quite right and fitting, and accept her destiny without the least nervous embarrassment.

In every recent American novel there is always an English peer, foolishly devoted to one of these fair enslavers, who snubs him or takes him, according to caprice, evidently of opinion that the favour is all on her side. In one novel, a peer, with an income of a hundred thousand a year, offers his hand, and is refused because he is only a weak, good-natured person, without that strength of intellect required by an American girl in her lover. All women are queens in America, and have no idea of recognising any social position as higher than their own. From men they exact the utmost homage ; indeed, the worship of women is the national religion, a sacred law and gospel that none dare infringe. Many types of face and feature may be found in the vast extent of America with its varied climate and diverse races, but the South and West are particularly rich in strongly - marked characteristics. The Mexicans are fine and handsome, with a mixture of Indian and Spanish blood, from which the women derive their superb hair and eyes and graceful figures, and the men their proud Hidalgo bearing.

The miners of the West are strong, bold and picturesque, as the men who may have led the Argonauts or founded Rome, and are worthy of their western land, which is a paradise of beauty, while every woman looks a Penthesilea or a brigand queen. The only one section of

America that is wholly deficient in personal beauty is the Mormon settlement. The Mormons own a glorious land, and are industrious and orderly, but the women, it is said, are of ideal ugliness of the colourless Saxon type, with white eyes and eyelashes, sandy hair and shapeless features. It is remarkable that not a single Irishwoman is to be found in the Mormon city, but the bright-eyed daughters of Erin have no objection to intermarry with the Chinese, who are always anxious to obtain Irish wives. Consequently a great colony of Hiberno-Mongolian origin is spreading along the border of the Pacific, and ethnologist will soon have a new type of humanity to study.

In New York there is no distinctive type of race—all races have been fused there into uniformity by the same habits, passions and ambitions, and the influence of Europe on society. The women are dressed by Paris and the men by London, and life is modelled on the English style, but with much more splendour of outlay and effect. New York is the true paradise of women, where they glow and glitter in their gorgeous plumage, while the men toil and work in their dusky offices to amass the wealth that may cover their wives with diamonds to startle Europe—a city of splendour, luxury and pleasure ; the third great capital of the world, and equal in wealth to London and Paris put together. Long after America had thrown off the political yoke of England, the bondage to English modes of thought still remained. The awe of England was upon the heads of the people, and social life, in consequence, was provincial and imitative, and wholly wanting in national individuality. America, in fact, was but a suburb of London, an infinite and colourless Bayswater. They did not dare to originate— they copied. They were fed on English ideas, affected English manners, and yearned to find some English ancestor of established lineage to whom they could affiliate themselves. Altogether they were prostrated in humble reverence at the feet of the mighty mother. But steam and the rapid facilities of travel have gradually weakened this awful homage to old social tradition. Modern America now laughs at ' the rusty, antiquated usages of England,' the rigid distinction of classes, the ridiculous ceremonials, the abject servility of the court life, with the bowings and backslidings of the gold-laced officials, so degrading, in the eyes of a republican, to freeborn humanity. And they mock also at the prosy,

I

dreary, respectable papers, their petty politics, their Hares and Rabbits Bill, and they weary of the dull routine of society, the vapid talk where no large free ideas are ever circulated, and no recognition is apparent of the great fact that democracy is sweeping down monarchy with all its antiquated ritual, to the moles and the bats. London, says an American writer, has two idols—Science and Royalty, and conversation fluctuates between the Electric Light and the last Foundation Stone laid by Royal hands. They find the English slow, ponderous, conventional. A people that would never startle (it would be bad form), who repress all individual assertion, and insist that everything should be done and said according to the custom and usage which has the force of law in English society. They notice the languid drawl of the English accent, the half-finished sentences, as if to complete an idea in the utterance would entirely bore the speaker with fatigue. The English, they say, speak nicely, but they do not know how to converse. They have no fluency, are crude and abrupt in expression, and quite infelicitous in smooth transitions. The girls are dull, diffident and monotonous, with their pale eyes, pale hair and sealskin jackets, one might gather a thousand, or fifty thousand of them together, and they would all be found precisely alike.

The American woman, on the contrary, disdains this colourless uniformity, and revolts against social usages that would limit her bold originality and assertive self-manifestation. She is proud, conscious, strong-souled and self-reliant. ' I am an American girl ' is answer enough to any timid old-world bigot. And this phrase expresses at once dignity, courage, self-respect and the independence of the emancipated republican. The English girl, in one of the novels, utters her little harmless platitudes in a soft, low monotone of broken sentences. ' How nice,' she murmurs, ' to have pictures on a rainy day—and it rains so often!' and so on, and so on, in a limpid, weak, watery way. Always shy and indistinct with her half-utterances, the stiff conventional attitude never changed, nor the level murmur illustrated by gesture or laughter. But the vigorous, vivacious American girl never omits a syllable; she speaks in a loud, clear voice, as if for the reporters, and as one worth hearing, who demands and extorts attention. She accentuates all she says with firm purpose and resolute determination to be heard. She is sharp, smart and terrible at re-partee, and may, perhaps, be sometimes fatiguing to the English ear with her voluble flow

of words. The English girl never stares, nor
asks questions with obtrusive curiosity. She
is trained to seem and to be a negation—a
dormant soul without volition or an opinion on
any subject, felt or expressed. Her American
cousin, however, has an agressive frankness,
based chiefly upon interrogatories and bold
personalities. Her gaze is clear and direct;
not 'the stony British stare,' but with the large,
truthful eyes of childhood—the eager, inquiring
glance of a candid nature. Truth is in all her
words. This Puritan virtue has indeed remained
an heirloom in the American family. They
have none of the subtle evasion and graceful
mendacities of high life in Europe—the delicate
flatteries, so charming and so false. These are
stamped out at once by the frank, fearless candour of the American girl. Yet one trembles
a little before a candour so uncompromising;
for we all shrink from the downright expression
of the actual, and the glare of an unshadowed
truth makes one nervous. But the Americans
have no mercy. Nature meant them for a
nation of interviewers. They generalise, describe and label you after ten minutes' inspection, and send off your portrait across the
Atlantic, with all your imperfections on your
head, for the amusement of the crowd, who

must be propitiated by a victim, and who applaud and shout, 'Bravo, Toro!' when a 'special' has been more than usually successful in tossing the victim from his horns, to be trampled in the dust of the arena. Yet they are by no means an ill-natured or cruel people; on the contrary, they are kind, generous and charming to the passing stranger who enters within their gates, but the Sovereign Demos has no reverence, and finds a subtle pleasure and sense of power in giving pain to sensitive natures; so, like Nero, they sometimes light their gardens with live torches for want of better pastime. They seem also to take pleasure in showing England that they are no longer held in bondage to English opinion; they have even suggested that their native language should in future be called American, not English; and they have already adopted a quite independent system of *orthografy*, from which all the superfluous letters are excluded.

It is not improbable, therefore, that a new dialect, which may be called Americanese, will be rapidly formed. Neologism is popular in America; they are perpetually adding new words to their vocabulary, borrowed, perhaps, from the Indians, or the Mexicans, or the Californian miners, or transmuted from the

Chinese dialects blended with Gaelic, which the Chinese colony learn from their Irish wives. So that when all these elements have properly simmered together for a reasonable time, the result will be a language widely different from the English of Addison and Ruskin.

Speech is a passion with the Americans. They orate at all times, and on all subjects, with a copious redundancy of expression that is startling to those accustomed only to the slow - moving, hesitating tongue of English speakers, who always seem painfully seeking for the next word, and finding it only by a happy chance after many efforts.

The Americans (men and women alike) are the most voluble of nations, and when trained are the most fluent orators. The women express their ideas with firmness, precision and perfect self-possession, and are admirable speakers on the platform. While men like Wendell Phillips, Doherty, Lowell, Boyle O'Reilly and others would have made their mark as orators in any assembly in the world. This gift of natural eloquence is due, perhaps, to the strain of Irish blood in their veins—for all men of note in America will be found connected, in some way or other, with the fluent, passionate Celtic race. The Saxon basis is the rough block of the nation; but it is the Celtic influence that gives it all its artistic value and finish. A recent President of the United States was the son of an Irishman; the great novelist, Henry James, is the grandson of an Irish emigrant; and the late Mayor of New York, also an admirable speaker, was an Irishman. Ireland has added not a little to the triumph of American genius, and America, in return, has often nobly flung her protecting banner over the desolate exiles.

The Americans are not remarkable as painters or musicians, but as actors, orators and writers they may take a foremost place in the world's pantheon. The power of expression by verbal symbols has certainly been given to them. Emerson is a study of thought crystallised into the most perfect forms; and the leading, living writers, in grace and charm of style, need not fear rivalry with the best English writers. We recognise at once in their work the artist touch, the care in composition, the purity of expression and the entire absence of the Zola element of degrading and degraded language, scenes and images. The American style is acute, fresh and exhilarating, full of quaint humour and gentle satire, which amuses without being malignant, and the pictures of social life, of the statesman and the journalist; the woman of the world, with her perfect grace and superficial culture; the fashionable girl, with her gossamer chatter; and the advanced woman, with her trenchant uterances, are all admirably sketched in the new novels.

We gather from these clever works the full expression of American life, with its strong desires, fierce rivalries, limitless rage for specu- lation, and energetic will to work, spend, enjoy and make the best of this poor mortal ex- istence, without wasting time on corroding thoughts over transitory pleasures.

Americans are not given to brood over the mysteries of life. They never question the universe for solution of the unknowable; they have no morbid melancholy, no divine dis- content, and never worry their heads over agnosticism, positivism or pessimism, but accept religion as it comes to them without any ques- tioning analysis, simply as part of the great whirl of work, dress and fashion, that makes up the sum of daily life.

They like reading, but not study. Everyone in the cars seems furnished with a sixpenny novel or magazine, while newspapers cover the land like snowflakes in midwinter; but above all, they like lectures, because they can thus combine easily acquired information with the excitement of dress and out-door variety, and a crowded lecture is infinitely more amusing than a solitary magazine; besides it is of importance to them to assimilate knowledge rapidly as they eat and live, for life with them is a feverish rush of excitement and enjoyment. They are rapid in speech, in travel, in speculation, in everything. They live, every moment of their lives, an intense, daring, crowded, audacious, reckless and restless life of work, wealth and luxury. The present is enough for them, they take each moment as it comes, and get all the good out of it they can.

There is no girlhood or boyhood; everyone is born grown up, and the life of self-assertion and speculation begins from the cradle. The young girls have perfect freedom at an age when Europe would not allow them out of the nursery. They receive gentlemen alone in the evenings, and go to theatres and public places with them, unaccompanied by any duenna; for the chaperone and lynx-eyed matron of old-world usage and tradition has been quite suppresssed in America, along with the superfluous vowels.

In America youth reigns supreme and unfettered, and there is little reference paid to parental authority. Young girls receive and

go out alone or with their male friends, as
fancy pleases, without any reference to the
unwritten law of tradition, which is of such
overwhelming force in Europe that to break
it would incur the ban of society.

Women in America, whether married or
single, rule society, and do not suffer society
to rule them.   They carry all before them
with imperial sway, and are the beautiful despots of the land. Fathers, brothers and husbands are at work all day in the fierce strife
and excitement of the ceaseless speculation,
which is the national form of gambling.   But the
men never interfere with the interior management of the house ; all the arrangements and
expenditure and machinery of social life are left
to the taste, judgment and discretion of the
wife.   The province of the husband is merely
to fling down the showers of gold, which the
fascinating better half spends right royally.

American women, too, are learned as well as
being admirable housekeepers. They can extract
square roots as well as pickle them, and think
no more of encountering the difficulties of Latin,
Greek, and all terrific ologies, than our ladies,
those of the crewel or Berlin work.

What, however, is of more consequence than
all these elaborate efforts to make women ugly

by making them learned—for has not Walter
Savage Landor said, that *thought* adds beauty to
a man, but takes it from a woman—is the study
of that art in which the beautiful Americanese
have attained already to a high perfection, the
en touto niko art for a woman, that of *dress.*

Yet, alas! that grace, intellect and French
tournure cannot make youth and beauty immortal. These fair and fragile Americans,
though possessing all, yet fade as quickly as the
night-blowing cereus, reminding one of Goethe's
pretty apologue, 'Why am I so evanescent, O
Zeus?' asked Beauty. 'Because I have only
made the evanescent beautiful,' replied the god.
And when youth, beauty, the flowers and the
spring heard that, they withdrew themselves
weeping from before the throne of Jupiter.
Early marriages are consequently much more
frequent in America than here, for at twenty
these fair destroyers are already in the *mezzo
cammin*, or even the *selva oscura*, and at twenty-
five they are but traditions. '*Mais jettons une
voile sur la passée*,' as the Frenchman remarked,
while placing a shawl upon one of these sad
legends of antiquity. But no matter how
many decades she may number, woman is
always the great ruling power of America, and
the American has become the representative

woman of the world. Not crushed down as in
Europe by old traditions of mental and legal
inferiority, but asserting her sovereign right to
equality, and to exact and receive the homage
of men. Queens of beauty, lavish and extravagant in all things, gorgeous in toilette, insatiable
of pleasure, surrounded by the costly luxuries of
often illimitable wealth, the women of fashion
bask in a changeless radiance of show and
glitter, for money is easily made, and if also
easily lost they care little; they enjoy while
they can, eat, dress, dazzle and delight; but
love is not by any means a leading interest in
the life of an American woman, and seldom is
scandal heard of in their social circle; for the
very freedom of social intercourse trains woman
to habits of self-reliance, and encourages so much
self-esteem that they are quite insensible to
flattery. They know all their perfections
thoroughly, and they accept all praise as only a
proper acknowledgment of their merits.

Besides, American life is carried on in a perpetual public glare. In their huge hotels and
boarding-houses, caravanseries, where hundreds
meet and feed and talk together, there is no
mystery possible; nor is it needed, for divorce is
so easily obtained that passionate dramas of
fatal love and remorse form no element in their

lives. If the marriage bond is found too gall-
ing, it may be broken at once with very little
trouble; no one minds these minor family arrangements. Whatever is legal is right; and
the divorced pair meet in society, each supplied
with a new partner, and they dance in the same
set with cool nonchalance, and sometimes even
valse together with all that supreme indifference
to harrowing sentiment which is the perfection
of good manners.

The young girls also, though allowed such
entire social freedom, are saved from any com-
promising entanglement by a certain consciousness of their own value. 'They are not
coquettes, and have more pride than vanity—
a dignity which permits no shadow of disre-
spect; and their genial camaraderie with the
other sex is often much more allied to friendship than to love. The passion of the American
woman is rather for dress, pleasure and display.
She loves to live in public, to lead and reign in
society. Notoriety is not displeasing to her,
and she attains it easily through the press,
for there are hundreds of writing women, though
but few really eminent names. Among leading
brilliant writers may be named Mrs Julia Ward
Howe, whose writings, both in prose and verse,
place her in the front rank of gifted women.

Her celebrated poem, *The Battle Hymn of the Republic*, is one of the finest lyrics of the age, and deserves a place in the literature of nations. In life and manner she is simple and unaffected. Her brilliancy is all of the intellect. Yet, even in her unpretentious Quaker dress, one can see that she has had remarkable beauty, which her daughter, one of the loveliest girls in America, has inherited.

Mrs Hodgson Burnett, though only a naturalised American, yet may be called an American writer. She was first known in England by her admirable novel, *That Lass o' Lowrie's*, of which thirty thousand copies were sold of the first edition. This was followed by her clever work, *Through One Administration*, a brilliant sketch of social, political and official life at Washington, drawn with sharp and rather satirical touches; but her popularity was assured by the success of *Little Lord Fauntleroy*, especially in its dramatic form.

An acute American critic remarks of Mrs Burnett,—'She understands suffering and sinning natures, and discovers gracious secrets in forbiding characters.'

Mrs Atherton of New York, one of the young band of female writers, has obtained considerable celebrity by her novels, especially by *Los*

Cerritos, an interesting and picturesque picture of rude Californian life amongst the squatters, with their strange idiom and fierce, lawless ways, all most vividly described. Another of the young writers, Amelia Reeves, is chiefly remarkable for a very lovely face, an unbridled imagination, with a total disregard of probability in her stories, and a wild, passionate fervour of eloquent expression.

Mrs Piatt, wife of the American Consul at Queenstown, Ireland, takes high rank amongst the poetesses of America. Her verse has great strength and beauty, and is always strikingly original, yet simply tender and sympathetic, especially when touching on the subject of children, or the poor and suffering. While Louise Chandler Moulton—a poet celebrity in London as well as in America—has set all the soft human emotions to music in her beautiful and cadenced verse. Both Tennyson and Browning extolled her genius, and Mrs Moulton is proud to remember them amongst her best friends.

Literary women hold a high place in American society, and receive more social homage, as a tribute to intellect, than is accorded to literary women in London. Their brilliant circles include all that is eminent in genius, and they inspire, and stimulate with generous praise and

true enthusiasm, all that is noble in mind or
work. Thus they form an important section of
society, and use all the immense power American women possess as social leaders, to uphold
the dignity of intellect by refined and high-
toned social intercourse. As social writers, they
do not indulge in the grotesque sarcasm which
so often disfigures the productions of the male
contributors ; and, as a rule, whatever is best
and most appreciative in the society journals
of comment or criticism may be safely attri-
buted to a female pen. The most important
and successful journalist in the States is a
woman—Mrs Frank Leslie. She owns and
edits many journals, and writes with bright
vivacity on the social subjects of the day, yet
always evinces a high and good purpose ; and,
with her many gifts, her brilliant powers of
conversation in all the leading tongues of
Europe, her splendid residence and immense
income, nobly earned and nobly spent, Mrs
Frank Leslie may be considered the leader and
head of the intellectual circles of New York.

In former times the Americans lived almost
entirely and piratically on English thought ; but
they are now producing a new and independent
literature, of which the style, tone and colouring
are quite removed and distinct from English

models. While, with regard to technical excellence, the type, paper, binding, illustrations, woodcuts and etchings, they seem far ahead of the old country. They have also brought to the very highest perfection the photographic art, of which Saroni's portraits are an admirable example. All the leading continental works, from Paris to Stockholm and St Petersburg, are translated at once, and in the best style ; while works by native writers on science, art, literature, history and archæology are beginning to appear in copious profusion. To these the current literature of England is added. Everything good is appropriated, though, it must be confessed, seldom paid for ; a serious injustice to English brain-workers. But the system at least spreads the fame of English writers ; while in England scarcely anything is known of the rich and varied literature of America. Hawthorne's *Scarlet Letter* first startled the English mind with a sense of the peculiar intellectual power of America ; but it is only recently that the eminent living novelists are becoming known to the reading public of England. A great deal of the popular writing (especially the journalistic) is certainly grotesque, personal and impertinent, reckless of giving pain, and wanting in good manners, reverence, reticence and

K

due consideration for others. It seems as if a
people that have ceased to fight for liberty still
need blood, and must have the arena and the
amphitheatre, the fierce lions of the Press, and
the victims who are interviewed and slain. In
the capricious chances of popular favour the
victim may certainly be sometimes crowned, but
is too often rent or stoned. The Americans are
fond of travel, though the childlike worship of
the Old World no longer exists. They have
begun to recognise their own immense advantages, and to find out that Europe is 'rather a
humbug'—a mummy, smothered in bandages
of old forms and formulas, that are but the
cerements of the dead. The tone of American
thought is colossal, their country is colossal, their
mode of living, expenditure, wealth and speculations are all of immense proportion. 'They consume twice as much of everything as any other
people on earth,' one of their own writers says.
It is not surprising, then, that Europe seems so
small to them, after the vastness of their own
horizon. The mountains, rivers and plains are
as nothing to them after their own, and 'the
baby-house scenery' of Europe fails to impress
people who have looked on the foam and heard
the thunders of Niagara. Even the Atlantic is
but a mere ferry in their eyes, and they think

no more of a run over to Europe than a Lon-
doner of a run down to Brighton. They laugh
at the little kings and kingdoms, and, in their
large, expansive way, speak of ' the Latin
countries ' generally, as if quite too insignificant
for separate notice.

' The Innocents Abroad ' are, in fact, ruthless
iconoclasts, and mock at legends and ruins,
rubbish and relics. They do not find the rail
cars as comfortable, the hotels as sumptuous,
the champagne as good as the American ; nor
the women as beautiful as those they left in
Baltimore and New York, while to American
women, accustomed as they are to admiration
and homage, European society seems dull,
heavy, monotonous and unappreciative. They
do not care to go ' moping about galleries or
churches.' They find Venice slow, and stories
of the Falieri rather a bore. They want life,
variety, fashion, amusement, picnics and pro-
menades—enjoyment, in a word; not guide-
books and routine. They are seeking material
for a smart letter to the journals, and they find
only formality and the police.

The female tourist is very amusingly drawn
in one of the recent novels. She does not care
for Turner's landscapes nor Assyrian bulls ; she
wants the present the actual humanity, not

fossil bones. Her fervent aspiration is to meet all the celebrities of London at a dinner-party, to note their peculiarities, faces and features, talk and movements, and then dash off a letter to the journals, with accurate descriptions, marked, no doubt, by all the terrible candour of American nature, which is never glamoured by an illusion, but goes right at the fact with fatal precision.

Americans are amazed at the blind devotion of Europe to the old grooves and the ancient idols of routine and form, apparently unconscious that the pillars of the temple are failing and falling, and that any day a crash may come. bringing down the whole superstructure, built on ceremonial and symbols that have lost their strength since they lost their meaning.

Yet the spell of England, 'mystic, mediæval England,' is upon them still ; and London has a charm for Americans beyond all classic Europe, as the origin of their nation, the founder of their laws, religion and social habits. 'Sombre London, the mighty mother of our mighty race,' as one of their writers finely designates the great capital of the English people, has an irresistible attraction for them. They love its pleasures and social crowds and stately court functions, with all the awful solemnity and the splendour of visible royalty.

Some even assert a liking for the shrouded atmosphere, the soft, moist air, the veiled skies, and the light, 'the ineffable English light,' so restful and soothing after the lurid glare and cloudless azure heaven of America. And the old homage to England is shown in an effort, which is decidedly in progress, to form an aristocracy after the English model, with titled distinctions.

The wives of officials are beginning to arrogate to themselves the prefix of 'Honourable,' if it belongs by right of office to the husband; and the wife of the next American Minister at London may, perhaps, require to be called 'Her Excellency.'

The movement, however, has no chance of success, for the good sense of the American public is entirely against it; and already the leading journals have denounced its absurdity, along with the liveries, the fourteen servants, the coat of arms, and the four horses of the Republican imitators of the vain glories of a monarchy.

An aristocracy is the growth of a thousand years' feudal lordship, when men had the power of life and death over their vassals; and the English aristos still retain the haughty habits of command, and are treated with traditional reverence, though the power and the feudal rights have passed away.

But an aristrocracy cannot be made at once out of men who rise from rude toil or sordid vocations, by dint of fierce competition in trade, or some lucky chance in striking oil.

The Americans should be content to remain as they are, the great republican expression of human progress ; where everyone stands on the same level, and is entitled to the same consideration ; where the rail-splitter may become the equal of kings, and the daughter of the dry-goods man take her place amid the nobles of Europe, and consider herself quite their equal.

The true dignity of America is in the brain power that has transformed a wild, waste continent into a splendid world of advanced civilisation by the stupendous energy and intelligence of working men.

The old - world nations have been for six thousand years painfully toiling from Ararat to the Atlantic to advance the standard of humanity, and still the triumphs of intellect over ignorance, misery and desolation are incomplete.   But in a hundred years the Americans have spread over half the world, furrowed it

with iron roads, spanned the mighty rivers,
driven paths through the mountains, covered
the desolate plains with flourishing cities, and
sent the full tide of civilisation from ocean to
ocean with a force and power that leaves the
old-world kingdoms far behind in the race of
progress.

The sixty millions of America are made up of
a wonderful medley of heterogeneous elements,
but they have all the one watchword 'Advance!'
They are recruited from the young blood of all
nations, for only youth and energy emigrate,
and they have the spirit, the courage and the
daring of their origin.

Thus the process of fusion goes on rapidly,
and already America is becoming strong and
assertive with the dignity of a united people.
There are no oppressed nationalities, all are
equal and have the same privileges, and all
uphold the republic with pride and affection,
and never dream of giving up the advantages
it offers to go back to the bondage of old-world
limitations and the chilling influence of class
prejudice.

It is remarkable how soon all races become
Americanised. No foreign language takes root
among them. In a generation foreigners forget their native tongue, and English — the

wonderful English language that seems made
for the universe — remains triumphant and
alone.

American women are not idle in the war of
progress against prejudice. They have taken
an advanced position in the strife for right and
justice, and demand for their sex perfect
equality with men—social, legal, professional
and political, the right to vote, and even to be
elected to Congress, and as they are always
terribly in earnest, and have an indomitable
will, no doubt they will gain all they demand.
And already the women of Europe are following their example. English law has recently
made vast concessions, and even English
society, prisoned as it is in routine, is making
praiseworthy efforts to cast aside many of the
stupid old conventions of our false humanity.

The English girl is not so 'dull and diffident' as America represents her. She is becoming inspired with a love of freedom and a
consciousness of her own mental power, and
claims a social, professional and political
equality with the other sex. The 'matron,'
hitherto thought so indispensable in society as
guide and protector, is becoming an obsolete
institution. The English girl is learning independence, and by earnest study, intellectual

training and serious life work, is fitting herself for a higher and nobler position in the social organisation than she has hitherto held. Thus she will attain to the self-reliance and dignity that make her American sisters so important as a social power, while at the same time they lose none of their fascination as women.

There is a powerful electric influence in American nature that draws all other nations into its current, and an amount of overflowing nervous energy that is irresistibly stimulating to all who come into contact with it.

The gates of empires cannot be closed against eternal principles, nor can they be warred against by material agencies.

The march of ideas is predestined. Especially when ideas mean a free career for talent, equal chances of work and wealth for all men and women alike, and the fall of ignorance and idleness before enlightenment and industry and education, for on these things the well-being of a people is founded, and the happiness of nations and of humanity.

THE WORLD'S NEW PHASES.

THE railroads of the world are fast becoming the truest and most reliable expression of national progress; and the intellectual advance in art, science and civilisation of any country or region of the earth can be estimated at once, and lead off clearly by a survey of these iron *oghams* cut deep on the surface of the globe. Along these grooves the thoughtful mind will be led in a thousand directions; for steam and electricity have transformed the world, and almost annihilated space and time. Europe is joined to America by bands of vapour and a coil of wire, while separate nationalities, once jealous of and hating each other, are becoming merged into one universal brotherhood, who claim the whole earth as their heritage and country; and all peoples and nations on the face of the globe are tending towards the realisation of the grand formula of an ideal future—Fraternity, Liberty and Equality for all

the children of men—a powerful, united, en-
lightened humanity.

Every child born now is heir to a wonderful
heritage of light and knowledge. Science is
daily discovering new and infinite sources of
wealth—special gifts lying latent in each
country, by which a people could become truly
prosperous if they only knew how to use them;
so that if poverty and degradation and misery
exist, it is man's sin and not God's curse, that
has brought these evils on any land.

Even in the last twenty years what changes
have been effected in the relations of nation
with nation, and in our knowledge of the vast
treasures awaiting human enterprise in every
portion of the globe. And what grand portals
are opening everywhere for the onward march
of humanity. France has made a path at Suez
for the ships of the world to pass from the
Mediterranean to the Indian Sea; while America
throws a railroad across Panama to connect the
two great oceans, the Atlantic and the Pacific;
thus realising the dream of Columbus of a direct
path from Europe to Asia by the *West;* for it
is proved now that the shortest route possible
from London to China lies along the great high-
way of the Atlantic, across Panama to the East
Pacific.

English enterprise also is developing a new and unthought-of region of fertility and beauty in the interior of Africa, where even the gentler sex brave all dangers for the sake of knowledge, and a woman's hand has helped to draw back the veil of Isis. Lady Baker, with only the torch of love to guide her across the mighty desolation of an untrodden world, aided to solve the mystery of the Nile; while Mrs Piazzi Smith, taking up her abode and making her habitation for months in an ancient Egyptian tomb, assisted her husband to take the measurement of the Pyramids. Then, America—colossal America—lying within eight days' sail of our Irish shores, sends on the poverty-stricken hordes of over-crowded Europe by its forty thousand miles of railway to regions where land is given them for the asking, and wealth is certain if they work. The human race is as yet but a handful on this magnificent continent, which God seems to have given to Europe just as Europe, effete and exhausted, failed in the resources adequate for the support of her own children. And American energy knows no limits ; railroads have been carried five hundred miles west of the Missouri, and across the Rocky Mountains, discovering illimitable wealth of coal and iron as they advance. Two lines of railway are even now swiftly running across the buffalo hunting-grounds of the Indians, driving Indians and buffalos before them, and leaving these prairies of the west ready for the planting, peaceful hand of the emigrant to turn them into the greatest pasture plains of the world. Thus every iron line is a symbol and a prophecy of progress, and the exponent of the power, life and energy of a people. On looking over the most recent maps we see at once that England has done her work splendidly with her iron forces. She exhibits a dense network of railroads; France the same; and Prussia nearly equals them. These black lines tell of the energy of the three great energising nations of Europe. Happy, prosperous, flourishing little Belgium presents a goodly number of the best organised railways in Europe ; and Italy, under the powerful inspiration of her new-found life, is already rivalling her great compeers, and has brought Florence within thirty-six hours of Paris. Spain languidly tries to move on the iron groove, aided by English hands and brains; but the nobler nations of the north, Sweden, Denmark and Norway, have already succeeded, notwithstanding the difficulties of the undertaking, in marking several suggestive black lines on the rugged surface of Scandinavia.

Russian policy is represented exactly by her railroads. Russia neither desires the stranger to visit her, nor her own children to leave her. Therefore, she has no branch lines running hither and thither over the immense flat surface of her infinite swamp ; but she stretches out one long, menacing arm from St Petersburg to Moscow, thence across a distance of eight hundred miles, and clutches Warsaw in her iron grasp ; and with a branch line to Berlin, and a few offshoots from this one main trunk, Russian enterprise in the matter of railways has an end. But Asia no longer puts her trust alone in elephants for the purpose of locomotion ; the steam engine has dethroned these sagacious monsters, and the scream of the railway-whistle through forest and jungle startles the tiger in his lair. A railroad runs across India from the coast to Madras, and from Bombay to Calcutta ; and from Calcutta to Delhi one can travel a thousand miles by rail without even changing carriages. New Zealand also has her railroads and her telegraphs, and by these the ancient land of the cannibal is fast becoming an advanced, civilised, fashionable place, where wealth is plenty as in London, and society *almost* as brilliant as at Paris.

Australia is already an old established country,

equal, if not superior to the mother land in all that riches can command and industry achieve. But there are some nations that still persistently refuse the gospel of the Iron Age. China, for instance, denounces railroads ; hates them ; forbids them ; won't have them at any price. She will make no iron grooves for the chariot-wheels of the stranger to run lightly in ; and Pekin trembles at the thought of these great highways for the nations to pass over. Turkey is quite behind the age in these matters also. But the Japanese are wiser ; and as they have already constructed very admirable steamers without any European aid, so they will soon have railroads everywhere made by their own hands to delight their own cunning little eyes.

Africa, with all its horrors of burning deserts and brutalised humanity, is yet bounded north and south by bands of civilisation ; and the French at Algiers and the English at the Cape run their railroads and erect their telegraphs, which will one day, no doubt, meet and clash and flash in the very heart of Africa, by the shores, perhaps, of the great Albert Nyanza itself, with a branch line for tourists to the Victoria Falls, which, it is said, equal Niagara in grandeur. But even more than steamships and iron roads, does the electric wire tend to draw all the nations of the earth into one great unity. The human race, in fact, is becoming like one vast sentient being, surrounded by an invisible but homogeneous nervous system through which thoughts flash simultaneously with the rapidity of lightning, and minds separated by whole continents and oceans can vibrate in unison at the same instant, as if men had acquired divine attributes and become omniscient and omnipresent. We pledge our friends in America at our feasts, and the response comes back to us before the sparkles have died upon the wine-cup. An eclipse takes place in India, and the account of it is read in London before the shadow and the darkness have quite passed from the sun. It is impossible for ignorance and isolation to continue much longer under the all-powerful influence of these new-found forces. Every stroke of the piston is the trumpet-note of progress, and the triumph of intelligence, power and knowledge over the foes that keep men prisoned and fettered in mental and physical degradation.

In glancing over the maps of the world, even a careless eye must be struck with the remarkable advance of geographical knowledge, which has now named almost every point of the earth's surface from the Poles to the Equator.

The great blanks on the face of the globe
marked 'unknown,' so pleasant to our childhood, because thereby we escaped the dire
necessity of learning by rote the names of a
harrowing list of chief towns, seated upon an
aggravating number of rivers, are rapidly filling
up. New Zealand has become a seeond England, mapped out with homely English names
that tell the tale of that wonderful and indomitable English enterprise which pervades the whole
world, diffusing through every clime and region
the arts, industry and language of the great
nation which rules over one hundred and fifty
millions of the people of the earth. The portals
of the ice-world have been unbarred by English
enterprise and the daring of heroic men, amongst
whom none have shown more splendid courage,
or achieved more in Arctic exploration, than our
own brave Irishmen. The names of Sir Leo-
pold M'Clintock, of Kellett, Sherrard Osborne
and Maguire are foremost amongst those who
flashed light on the polar mystery, making
visible every cape and bay and headland along
the utmost limits of the earth ; while another
gallant Irishman, Sir Robert M'Clure, solved
the problem of the North-West Passage, and
sailed his ship triumphantly from the Pacific
round by the north coast till within sight of

the waters of the Atlantic ; but there, blocked
up by ghastly walls of impenetrable ice, he
seemed destined to add his name to the fatal
list of Arctic discoverers, while day by day for a
thousand days he and his crew watched the
ice closing round their doomed ship, as in the
old Spanish story we read of the prison walls
contracting, by some secret mechanism, round
the victim within till they crushed him to death.
So three years passed, till all hope failed, and
they stood face to face with death as only brave
men can.   They nailed their flag to the mast and
resigned themselves to die ; but at that last
hour relief came like a miracle—a ship was
at hand to rescue them.   And the most affect-
ing scene ever witnessed perhaps under the
polar sky was when the two friends, the two
Irishmen, M'Clure and Kellett, one having
sailed by the Pacific, and the other by the
Atlantic, met and clasped hands on that lonely
ice-field, and M'Clure, kneeling down, thanked
God for the tidings which saved him and his
companions from a horrible death.   But his
good ship, *The Investigator*, could not be freed
from the ice-fetters, and had to be left to fate.
She may be in existence yet, with her flag still
floating in the silent polar air, though no human
eye may ever rest again on the spot named

by Sir Robert M'Clure, in memory of his great deliverance, 'The Bay of Mercy.' But it has taken its place permanently on the map of the world, and in the heroic but terrible annals of Arctic discovery.

And science ever follows quickly on the track of the explorer, revealing for mankind the utility and value of the new territories gained from waste and desolation, just as the information is most needed for the purposes of commerce and colonisation. If the rumour goes forth that the resources of the Old World are failing—that the coal of England is nearly exhausted, and her stores of copper and tin are being brought low—then science announces that Australia possesses copper enough to supply the whole world, and that the coal-fields of America are inexhaustible.

If the human race is overcrowding this out-worn Europe, then science lifts the veil from the centre of Africa, and shows a lofty table-land fit for all the purposes of life—with green pastures, lakes as large as all Scotland, lofty mountains pouring down eternal cataracts to feed that mighty river, the Nile, which traverses 36 degrees of latitude, or the fifth part of the entire distance from pole to pole—a magnificent new world, containing millions of square miles, given over to the despairing European, who fights through life and death for the possession of one acre of land at home.

If the pasture lands of Europe are proving insufficient for the increasing population, then science drives her rail-car through the boundless prairies of the West, clearing a path through regions where millions might live, and feed the whole world besides. London now makes its marketing at New York, and every nation and people will soon be bound together by that strongest bond and pledge of peace and unity, mutual necessity and mutual advantage.

But science, though it has revealed many facts, has not yet solved all mysteries, and the early condition of our globe is still one of these mystic problems. It is supposed that the earth was once an immense unbroken plain, with a climate very different from the present, for it is proved that tropical verdure once reigned at the north, and that the present lands of snow were then fair lands of flowers. Recent explorations of Greenland show that a rich tropical vegetation once existed there ; and Sir Robert M'Clure found traces of petrified forests at the extreme end of the polar world, where not a shrub will live now. This vast elder world was then, it is thought, broken up and dislocated

into continents; two oceans separated the earth
into two hemispheres; islands were flung off
from the mainland; the British Isles were rent
from Germany; Ireland was torn from the coast
of Spain, where the Bay of Biscay now flows;
New Zealand was hurled by volcanic action
from that region of volcanoes, the Pacific coast
of America, and remains to this day a volcano
itself, or rather an aggregate of volcanoes, with
fountains of steam and rivers of boiling water;
and so all other changes went on—by which
mountains rose, and lake and river and sea
were formed—till the world settled down quietly
into its present condition. But, amidst all these
changes, Africa — according to Sir Roderick
Murchison—suffered no mutations and shows
no sign of submersion or dislocation, or of
volcanic action, but remains, in the midst of
a new order of things, a fragment of an elder
primitive granitic world, the oldest portion of
our globe; while America he pronounces to be
the latest and newest—a modern alluvial plain
—a region of volcanoes and earthquakes, as if
scarcely yet settled down into compact solidity.

Europe, the most highly-favoured portion of
the globe, owes all its wealth, power, commerce
and salubrity of climate to this dislocating process. Every rift of the ocean, every cleft of

the mountain, made a path for knowledge, or revealed a source of wealth ; while Africa, which admits the ocean nowhere, has remained till now impervious to all commerce and civilisation, except at the coast.

Science has also penetrated the depths of the ocean, and told us of that immense sub-Atlantic plain—perhaps the submerged surface of an elder world—where for a thousand miles a car might run without meeting an obstacle to its progress. And, lifting its glance to the sun, science has analysed its substance, revealed the metals it contains—above all, the abundance of iron, from which the inference may be drawn that life there is not radically dissimilar from our own—that it also has its needs and requirements, and that intellect akin to the human, though probably far loftier and nobler, has the same material objects to work on to supply them.

But the history, the orgin, the duration of that early mystic race of man, whose remains are strewn over the surface of the earth, are problems which not even science has yet solved. Who can tell the origin of this great, silent race, that has not left one written sign or symbol of human speech, though its footsteps can be traced from farthest India to the last headland of western Ireland, and from thence across the great plains of America by that mysterious alpbabet of stone which yet none can form into intelligible words to tell us whence they came or whither they went. A mighty race indeed, that has left ineffaceable memorials of its world-wide wanderings. Recent discoveries in the valley of the Mississippi alone show a space of upwards of a hundred miles covered with their grave-mounds, while the soil is rich with quantities of their peculiar stone implements, identical in form and fashion with those found in Ireland, specimens of which are exhibited in such profusion in our Royal Irish Academy.[1] Many hold the belief that this people of the Stone Age was an antediluvian race which perished in the great catastrophe of the Deluge ; while others have supposed for them a pre-Adamite origin. This theory of a series of pre-Adamite races, gradually completing the links of the chain between the lower animal and intellectual man, has received additional confirmation from the recent explorations in Central Africa. There we find a race hideous in all respects, morally and physically—revolting to all human senses —without any notions of a God, of a moral law,

[1] For a full description of these implements see the 'Catalogue of Antiquities' of the Royal Irish Academy, by Sir William Wilde, Vice-President, R.I.A.

of truth or justice, or any rule of life beyond
what cunning teaches—without memory, or
history, or traditions, the first link apparently
between the gorilla and man—differing only
from the brute creation by the gift of speech.
And so they have remained for at least six
thousand years, fragments of an elder race,
as Africa itself is of an elder world; shut up
from all human intercourse or chances of improvement by bands of desert and a cordon of
poison. But for what purpose in God's great
providence this horrible destiny was laid on
them, none can know.

The men of the Stone Age, on the contrary,
show a comparatively high organisation; for
they have left evidences of ingenuity and design,
of a sense of symmetry and fitness, and proofs
of the adaptation of means to ends; and also of
a noble reverence for the dead, which almost
proves their belief in immortality.

But the most mysterious of all existing races
is the Chinese. This people that never knew a
childhood—that ever since human history began
has exhibited a knowledge of science and a
perfection in art which Europe even now cannot
equal. A nation that numbers three hundred
and fifty millions of people, whose language is
more spoken than any other on the face of the

globe, and to whom the tenth part of the earth
has been given for a possession. Yet, endowed
as they are with the keenest intellect, they are
morally but half developed. They have never
received, and are never likely to receive, the
great Gospel of Christianity ; they have never
been brought under the law of its blessings,
promises or judgments. And so they, too,
stand on the earth, a race apart; and have so
stood for six thousand years, strangers to that
fold within which alone, we are taught to believe
eternal safety and salvation can be found.
Some writers, from the peculiar nature of
Chinese intellect, so matured yet so unprogres-
sive, assume that the Chinese race is the latest of
the pre-Adamic races ; while others fancy they
have discovered in the Chinese the descendants
of Cain, to whom, we know from Scripture, the
knowledge of the higher arts, such as architecture, metallurgy and music, was first revealed.

For the leaders of humanity, however, we
must look to Europe. Someone has said,—
' The men of divine instincts are all European ;
and in Europe we find two races who are pre-
eminently the world-leaders—the Gothic or
Teutonic race, of which England is the highest
representative ; and the Celtic, including the
Latin, of which France is now chief and head.

These two races—the Teuton, grave, wise and industrious ; the Celt, brilliant, powerful and proud—seem destined to rule the world. The English language, the most perfect form of Teutonic speech, is now spoken by above two hundred millions of people ; English laws, literature, commerce, arts, manufactures and religion, extend over the whole of America, of Australia, of New Zealand, over half of Africa and half of India, and are permeating every seaport and every remotest island and country on the face of earth or ocean. Then to the Celtic race is given the finest portion of Europe —the Mediterranean shore with all its noble kingdoms, France, Italy, the Spanish Peninsula, Greece and the Ægean Isles ; the North of Africa is theirs ; their influence directs Egypt, has overleaped the wall of Chinese prejudice and is even felt in Japan ; whilst the *union* of the two races has formed, what promises to be the mightiest dominion the world has ever yet seen—the great American Republic. Celt and Teuton have met there in the strength of their united intellect and power, and no other race on earth can now hope to rival or conquer them. They are the great levers of humanity. Other races are stationery or retrogressive ; they alone advance. For them the law of life is onward. And the result will be to build up a better and a nobler humanity. Light and knowledge must follow in the path of the explorer—in the track of the iron car, and the missionaries of science will become the missionaries of God. And it is remarkable how rapidly all other tribes and nations that stand in the way of these two great destined races are disappearing from the earth—the half-souled Negro, the Red Indian of the prairies, the miserable Gnomes that guard the portals of the gold lands of the Pacific, as well as the luxurious, sensuous Oriental. The world is completing the cycle of its destiny, and travelling back to that era when all the earth was of one family, one speech, and one religion.

But through all the whirl of the world's changes and phases, let us see what has been doing for Ireland. Alas! we have no page to add to the great book of progress—no record of advance, only of decadence or stagnation! In three decades we lost three millions of our people—that is all we have to tell. Italy in that time has risen to a great, free nation of twenty-four millions; Greece, with a population of only a million and a half, has become a self-governed, independent State; Prussia has taken her place almost at the head of Europe; and Spain has

boldly asserted the right of a people to choose
their own form of government. We only dream
while others act :—

> ' The sounds we hear of the new Evangels,
> Rising like incense from Earth's green sod,
> But we alone, before worshipping Angels,
> Idly stand in the garden of God.'

With a population numbering twice that of
Switzerland, nearly four times that of Greece,
and equal to all Sweden, Norway and Denmark
put together, Ireland is still held in leading-strings
by another people ; and after fifteen hundred
years of Christian civilisation, and seven hundred
of British rule, we are still without commerce,
without literature, without a flag, without dignity
—in a word, without self-government. The
centre of Ireland is as unreclaimed as the centre
of Africa ; with a splendid sea-board, we are
still without passenger ships to take us to the
Continent, and are obliged to traverse the whole
breadth of England to find a vessel to convey us
to the adjacent coasts of France and Spain—
though ages ago, long before England set her
foot here, a constant and direct intercourse was
kept up between Spain and Ireland ; the magnificent West, which should be the great high-
way between Europe and America, with ships
on the ocean and rail-cars on the land to carry
on the traffic of two worlds, is still a silent,

solitary waste. Are we not, indeed, the true
lotos-eaters, described by Tennyson in a picture
he must have meant for Ireland :—

> In the afternoon they came unto a land
> In which it seemed always afternoon ;
> A land where all things always seemed the same,
> And round about the keel with faces pale
> The mild-eyed, melancholy lotos-eaters came ;
> And deep asleep they seemed, yet all awake.

Yet, through all fate and misfortunes, Ireland,
as part of the great Celtic race, is fulfilling the
great destiny of dispersion, and going forth to
possess the world.

This little island, scarcely larger than a good-
sized American farm, yet which her people allow
other hands to rule, is now but the expression of
the centre, not of the circumference of the Irish
nation ; for the Irish have founded a nation in
America and another in Australia already equal
in number to the nation at home. *Planetai*,
ceaseless wanderers through space, yet ever
turning with thoughts of affection round the one
common centre—their own old country.

It is remarkable that although the Irish
generally began life abroad at the base of the
social pyramid, they rapidly rise to the summit :
and while the solemn, industrious Teuton races
continue to plod on at the rough hard work of
the world, the daring, brilliant, ambitious Celt

aspires to lead and rule. Thus the Irish element is found strong in every civilised government except their own.

Our wanderings might lead us on over the maps of the world to an infinite of thought and speculation ; yet even from this brief survey the conviction must arise upon every mind that a brighter future is opening for the human race ; that light is gaining upon darkness, knowledge achieving her peaceful, yet stupenduous victories for man, and freedom is everywhere annihilating the system of the old feudal tyrannies, which kept the masses debased and abject in the bonds of ignorance and serfdom.

The Spirit of the Age goes forth conquering and to conquer, with its three mighty forces : Σοφια, δύναμις, νοῦς—Wisdom, Power and Mind ; revealing, destroying, reconstructing and building up a fairer world and a nobler humanity over the lair of the lion, the trail of the savage, and the wrecks and sediment of the bygone ages.

THE DESTINY OF HUMANITY.

NO speculative subject excites more intense interest at the present day than the future of the human race, especially in relation to those other planets of the great solar system, within whose stern and changeless laws our earth and all the planet worlds are alike inflexibly bound.

Perhaps we have been over-wearied with merely mundane knowledge, and feel the need, as it were, to search the infinite for new subjects of investigation. Curiosity has been satiated here. We know all about the physical condition of the earth, as it has been existing under many mutations for the last ten millions of years or more ; everything has been analysed and discussed and proved and tested in the alembic of science, till there are no more mysteries left of the visible world to excite the imagination, or to stimulate research for some yet undiscovered truth. But there is still one awful and gloomy mystery of the invisible world connected with our race which remains

unread. The generations pass in endless succession through the silent gate of death—the
wise, the learned, the noble, the good, disappear
in the fathomless abyss, and we, standing on
the brink in tremour and bewildered fear, await
the coming of the Fates—

> Dark-coloured queens, whose glittering eyes are bright
> With dreadful, mournful, life-destroying light—

yet vainly ask of revelation or philosophy for
some voice through the silence, some word from
the infinite, to tell us if there are other worlds
where the soul's energy will find a wider sphere,
and the divine intellect still more glorious
objects for its splendid powers than it finds on
earth.

No proof, however, has yet been found of the
existence of inhabited worlds beyond our own,
although dim previsions exist in most men's
minds that the planets are connected with the
history of humanity, both as past and future
abodes of the human race, through an endless
progression of intelligence in ever-changing
forms ; and when at night we look into the
fathomless star-depths of the infinite, we yearn
to know if the spirits of those we loved and lost
are dwelling above in some bright world where
life is nobler and more beautiful than it is on

our sorrow-stricken earth ; yet that even there, so far removed from sin and sorrow, some tender chord of human love may still vibrate in their nature, in sympathy with the tears that dim our eyes as we look upward and think of them, with the tender memories that can never die.

This question of life in other worlds, which has such a mystic and powerful attaction for all reflecting minds, first attracted popular attention from the eloquent and emotional manner in which it was treated by Chalmers in his astronomical sermons, and afterwards by the splendid utterances of Whewell and Brewster, in their celebrated essays, ' The Plurality of Worlds,' and ' More Worlds than One.'

In the former, Dr Whewell, the great antagonist of the habitation theory, maintains that our earth is probably the only abode in the universe fitted for rational beings ; and of the planets he affirms, that no other except our world has the conditions necessary to highly organised beings. The inner planets are globes of fire ; the outer are globes of water and frigid vapour, with scarcely any solid nucleus which could give the means to support life. The moon is a burnt-out cinder, without sea or atmosphere, where the wretched inhabitants, if

M

any existed, would be scorched with intolerable heat, then frozen with intolerable cold, every alternate fortnight.

The sun—that glorious orb which nations have worshipped as a god—he affirms, is nothing more than a gigantic fiery furnace of red-hot vapour, where life of any kind would be impossible; and the planets are incomplete worlds filled with inorganic material, or, if any organic creatures exist there, they could be only like the first evidences of creation in the slimy productions of the earth's earliest youth, before man appeared.

In Jupiter, for instance, they could be nothing more than fishy, flabby, boneless, gelatinous, hideous creatures, groping their lives out in a twilight of fog and watery vapour, through which the sun would appear merely as a speck of light.   And   one   could   scarcely imagine such beings endowed with conscious intelligence; while the planets Uranus and Neptune must exist in that 'outermost darkness' which is the Scripture expression for hell, intensified in horror by the duration of their winters, which in Uranus last for forty years, and in Neptune for eighty years, of a human life. Then, in the inner planets next the sun, no life or vegetation could sustain a heat seven times greater than that of our earth, where even metals would be reduced to a state of fiery vapour. The earth alone, according to his view, has a sufficient solid nucleus to support life—an atmosphere, a temperature and succession of seasons favourable to the manifestation of rational industry and intellect, and the enjoyments suited to a fine and highly sensitive organisation.

In opposition to these theories of Dr Whewell, Sir David Brewster maintains with great eloquence, and arguments drawn both from science and religion, that the omnipotent Intelligence could suit the organisation to the abode, and that the presumption of rational life throughout the solar system is great, from the evidence of compensation to the outer planets for diminished solar light, by the arrangement which supplies them with many moons, and Saturn with a resplendent ring of circling satellites ; and he asks,—' Could it be believed that through the millions of years of the protozoic and pre-human periods of the world's existence, before man was created, there was not to be found, a single rational being in the whole great universe of God ?'

Mr Proctor, a most brilliant writer on these subjects, takes a middle course, and his clear,

definite views, enforced with spirit and keen
argumentative power, deserve the deepest attention. He believes that rational life is a scarce
and rare phenomenon in the universe, not existing simultaneously in all the worlds, but manifested occasionally, and then lost, to reappear
again when the physical conditions have been
reached in other worlds, by which alone rational
life, as we know it, can be sustained. The compensation theory he refutes, by showing that the
moons of Jupiter scarcely afford any light to
their primary, owing to their great distance
from the sun ; and that the ring of Saturn
actually darkens the planet, in place of en-
lightening it, during half the year.

According to his theory, all the worlds and
suns of the universe pass through successive
and progressive stages during immense periods
of time. At first they are simply accretions of
burning vapour, which gradually attract to
themselves floating material of planet-forming
elements ; and, as they cool down, a solid
nucleus is formed, and organic life of the
lowest type begins to appear. Higher grades
follow in succession, but at long intervals, until,
finally, a race of beings gifted with conscious
intelligence, such as the human, takes its destined place as head and ruler of a perfected world.

Our earth, through millions of years, has been passing through all the progressive stages of formation and completion, until the culminating moment arrived when the highest product of development was manifested in man ; but that was only six thousand years ago, so brief is the history of intelligence in the history of worlds. And already the earth is showing signs of decrepitude and lessening vital power. Worlds, like living creatures, have their fiery youth, their full, calm maturity, and their failing age and final death.

Nothing remains steadfast in the universe ; all things fluctuate and change. Even the sun is in a process of exhaustion, so that eventually life will fail on the earth, directly by the decay of vital force, and indirectly by the dying out of the solar heat and light which is the source of all planet life ; and this world at last will become silent and lifeless, a bleak and barren waste, as the moon is at the present moment.

The progress of civilisation, he adds, is also rapidly consuming the earth-wealth by which men live. The great forests are disappearing from above the soil, and the great coalfields from beneath it. It has been even calculated that in five hundred years the coal will be extinct—a mere moment in the history of a world, but a moment that will bring consequences of awful import to humanity, for either an entirely new order of things must be established on this earth within the next thousand years for the human race, or the human race itself will perish and become extinct.

Meanwhile, however, other worlds are preparing for the reception of rational beings, and, according to Mr Proctor, Jupiter, Saturn and the outer planets are even now passing through the fiery stage, which is the azoic period of all worlds, and from which they rise into abodes fit for rational life.

The objection to the possibility of life existing in the remote planets by reason of their immense distance from the sun, he meets by the hypothesis that they are not dark, opaque masses revolving in space, like our earth, but self-luminous suns, lighting up the otherwise thick darkness of the outermost regions of the solar system.

He holds, for instance, that Jupiter, the largest planet of the system, in place of being a huge ocean of fog and mist, is a globe of fiery vapour, giving resplendent light and heat to his circling moons, which are the inhabited portions of the Jovian system, if there be inhabitants, and which revolve round their primary in the warm glow of an endless spring.

Saturn, in like manner, is a mass of incandescent vapour, giving light and heat to his attendant moons, and to that lustrous ring of countless satellites, so massed together that they seem like one continuous arch of light.

Yet, a time may come when these fiery suns will absorb into their masses the circling satellites, and as the minor worlds are accreted a solid nucleus will be formed as a basis for supporting a new phase of life; the life of the satellites will then gradually die out, but in their place new and splendid worlds will be formed, fitted for the abode of those higher races for whom alone all worlds exist.

These daring theories of a mind, which seemed to see by inner vision the formation, life and death of worlds and sun and systems, are supported by the argument that, as far as our earth is concerned, we know from scientific investigation that the azoic inchoate state of the world lasted for millions of years, while it was passing from the condition of fiery vapour to that of a concrete mass, but six thousand years cover the brief period of its human, historic life; from which Mr Proctor concludes that 'the lifeless gaps in the history of the solar system far exceed the periods of life with which they alternate.'

From this view of the succession of vital epochs it seems not improbable that it is our own human race which is destined to pass through all the changes of life and death and resurrection, from world to world of the eight planets connected with the solar systsm ; so that in place of there being a distinct creation, and a new race for each planet, it is humanity itself, ever dying, ever living, that will travel from star to star, from grade to grade, still ascending in the infinite scale of power, intelligence, beauty, and moral harmony, until the human becomes almost divine, and reaches at last the glorious promised Heaven within the radiant, central temple of the sun.

It is right to state, however, that in Mr Proctor's theory, the sun is not a habitable world. He considers it as being now only in the first stage of all worlds, that of a mass of burning vapour. Yet others, and not without reason, believe that the sun fulfils exactly that splendid dream of Heaven pictured for us in the sublime description of the seer of Patmos—a glowing world of light and of eternal summer, where there is *no night*. Of no other body in the solar system can this be predicted. Of the sun alone it is true ; there can be no night as he revolves in the unchanging light of his own luminous atmosphere, and for the same reason, no change of seasons. No seed time or harvest ; eternal summer must reign for ever there, and the Tree of Life will grow beside the living waters, as the trees by the rivers of Paradise.

' No night' implies also that stated periods of repose after toil for weary workers, and frail, decaying organisms will not be needed; these are the conditions of labour and of imperfect frames that require constant renovation through sleep. For the perfect organism, not subject to disease or death, there will be eternal youth, without the weariness of exhaustion, or that decadence of vital power which we call old age.

These views are not altogether fanciful : such conditions must exist to some extent in a world where there are no seasons for toil and no nights for rest ; and sorrow could hardly find place in a world where youth, beauty, peace and joy, and the divine powers of the intellect were eternal, and subject to neither exhaustion nor decay. The inspired writer describes such a world and calls it Heaven, and one cannot lightly cast aside the belief that the sun may be that destined and glorious home of our race where ' the nations who are saved shall walk in light.'

The splendour of the vision is even increased by the recent discoveries of science, which show the magnificence of the spectacle that surrounds the sun. Pillars of light formed of luminous gas, spring up vertically on every side to an enormous height like the mighty columns of a temple, then fall down again on the sun like the spray of a fountain, and there assume the forms of gigantic trees rich in branches and dazzling foliage, until gradually the whole magnificent mass sinks down in soft clouds upon the solar surface.

The intense heat, which would make life insupportable, is modified, some philosophers think, by a veil of mist, which, rising from the ground high above the solid nucleus of the sun, forms a majestic dome, beneath which might dwell in safety the glorified races of all the worlds ; and it has been supposed that the dark spots seen on the sun are openings in this dome, through which the inhabitants can behold the outer firmament, and the philosophers of earth behold the dark solid body of the sun.

But the sun also, with all its attendant planets, is moving swiftly through the star-depths to some unknown point, where, perhaps, in the far distant ages, the whole solar system will be absorbed by some system still more stupendous, and new cycles of life will commence, of a splendour and power of which the darkened soul of humanity can now form no conception.

The star Sirius, for instance—' the giant sun,' as Mr Proctor calls it—a thousand times larger than the sun of our system, may be the centre to which all worlds are tending, and the centre now of worlds where the inhabitants have a destiny of felicity and perfection of intellect, unknown to our limited, dark and blind and storm-tossed existence.

But, however mighty in power and intellect may be the inhabitants of the worlds revolving within the splendours of the magnificent Sirius, they must, in all important points that characterise rational beings, be akin to the human.

It has been proved that the same laws of motion and force, of heat, light, electricity, gravitation, attraction and repulsion pervade the infinite. The Omnipotent Ruler of the universe rules through unchanging physical laws; and the moral laws which guide, control and direct the actions of all rational existences throughout all the worlds, must be as unchangeable and universal as the laws of matter; for the moral

nature of man is a manifestation of the moral
nature of God, and, therefore, unchangeable in
its essence, and eternal in its unity with the
divine mind.

There can be no world, however distant,
throughout the infinite, where justice, truth,
love, mercy, purity, and all that makes human
life most beautiful, are not recognised by
rational beings as the highest law and rule of
life. As Kant has said, — ' The command,
" Thou shalt not lie," is not valid for man alone.
It is for all rational beings as well as man; for
the basis of obligation is not in the nature of
man, but *à priori* in the conceptions of pure
reason ; and so are all moral laws.'

And this thought infinitely ennobles the
human race. We are one in nature with all the
intelligences of the universe ; the difference, as
regards power of intellect and holiness of will,
may be quantitative, but is not qualitative.
Man's life seems no longer mean and isolated ;
it is an arc in an infinite circle, comprehending
all life that draws its being and nature from the
divine. Even the identity of the elements that
form all the worlds has been demonstrated by
the spectroscope, and revealed to us through
the language of light and colour.

We now know that iron and all the metals

familiar to earth are found in the planets and in the sun, and with the same properties. Iron especially has been proved to exist in enormous quantities in the sun, so that we may consider it to be an immense magnet suspended in space. But it is worthy of note, that although, from the apocalyptic vision, we are accustomed to associate the idea of the sun with the radiant city—the new Jerusalem—the central temple of our system, whose pavement is of gold, and whose walls are of precious stones, yet the presence of gold amongst the elements that form the mass of the sun has not hitherto been detected.

From the unity of material throughout the worlds of space, we may infer that the modes of utilising it in some manner analogous to the industries of earth exist there also; and, rising still higher, we may infer, from the unity both of material and of law throughout the infinite, the existence of one Supreme Intelligence, all-wise, all-powerful, who has ordained and organised all, and given the initial force which keeps the ever-moving, ever-steadfast machinery of the universe in eternal and unerring order.

In Mr Hamilton's interesting and instructive work, *The Starry Hosts*, the question of the habitation of the planets is discussed very ably, and with much convincing force, from a religious point of view. It is, indeed, impossible to approach the subject of astronomy except in a religious spirit. The evidences of infinite wisdom and power are so overwhelming, the scheme of the universe so vast, yet so perfect in its obedience to law, that none but the fool could say in his heart, ' There is no God.'

> ' There dwells a noble pathos in the skies,
> That warms the passions, proselytes our hearts.'

The awful beauty of the star-crowned night, the sublime magnificence of the fathomless infinite of revolving worlds and suns, compel the spirit to adoration, while at the same time we feel with deeper intensity our own high prerogative as a portion of the all-pervading intelligence that fills the universe, deathless in essence, though manifested in ever - changing forms. A great poet has said :—

> ' At night an Atheist half believes in God.'

And at such moments the well-known words of Kant may rise to the memory with a fuller sense of their sublimity :—' Two things fill the mind with ever new and increasing admiration and awe, the oftener and the more steadily we reflect on them—the starry heavens above, and the moral law within.'

And there is truly a striking analogy between the two, for all these revolving unresting
worlds are incessantly acted upon by opposing
forces, one driving them to chaos, the other
drawing them to total absorption within the
burning mass of the primary. Yet, from the
perfect balance of the tangential and centri-
petal forces, they are forced to move in that
steadfast and harmonious curve round the
primary, which, through millions of years,
remains unaltered.

So it is with the soul acted on by the opposing forces, the carnal and the spiritual, and
which finds its steadfast path alone in the
mean, or the μεσότης, of which Aristotle speaks
as the highest rule of life—the balance of the
dual nature of man between the life according
to reason and the chaos of a life according to
the senses.

And as the worlds of space never traverse
the same path twice, but are ever drawn on
with their primaries in an endless spiral towards
some unseen, far distant point, so the soul takes
a new standpoint at every step of its infinite
progression, and is destined never again to
know the path or the past it has once left.

It is along these lines of thought we are led
by the earnest, believing tone of Mr Hamilton's

book. No proof can be given that the planet worlds are inhabited; and he does not attempt a proof. It is a great 'perhaps,' no more, but the arguments he uses from reason, from our knowledge of the Divine mind as revealed to us in Scripture, and from the intuitions of our own nature, are even more convincing to many minds than those based upon scientific data. For science goes but a short way along the shrouded path of infinite mystery, and can affirm only with a hesitating asseverance what may be afterwards overthrown by wider views and more perfect knowledge of the physical world.

His work, though showing a wide knowledge of astronomical details, is yet quite free from technicalities, and therefore well suited to the general reader and to young persons, who are often deterred from the study of astronomy by the dry array of figures, fearful and incomprehensible, which beset their path, whereas the question of life in other worlds is one rather to be apprehended by feeling than demonstrated by mathematical calculations. He agrees with Mr Proctor in the belief that the vital epochs in the universe are not simultaneous, but successive, and manifested only at long intervals. But his faith is greater, and he affirms from spiritual insight, where Mr Proctor only hazards a conjecture, derived from analogy. He recognises, also, the unity of matter and the universality of law, but he makes no attempt to define the forms or modes of existence of the planet races ; he only claims for them conscious intelligence and a moral nature—that they are beings, therefore, who can show forth the glory of God through the intellect, the will, and the affections.

The question is one which has an immense influence upon the human mind, for if we believe in the eternal relation of all intelligences with each other and with God, the notion of annihilation after death becomes untenable and impossible. The universe, then, seems to us like an infinite harp—strike one chord, and all vibrate in unison—and we feel that man was not brought into this wondrous sphere of conscious being merely for this world and for this one brief life ; the whole planet system is his kingdom, and the whole universe is to him a consecrated temple, where, by right of his deatehlss intellect, he holds an eternal place. All progression is towards perfection, and, in these other worlds, man, gifted with divine strength and clothed upon with a more glorious vesture, may find the antagonism between the higher and lower nature gradually become less and less, until at last the harmony between the will of man and the law of God is perfected, and the ideal heaven of peace and blessedness is reached.

Yet, in spite of this community with the universe, it seems the destiny of the human soul to be eternally alone. A crystal wall insulates and separates each one from his race, and even from his nearest kindred. There are despairful moments in life, when it seems as if we stood alone in the universe. We gravitate towards no centre—have no place in any system—and the primitive force which flung us into being seems ever hurling us onward and downward into an infinite depth of darkness, silence and utter loneliness. No heart reveals itself fully to another; no soul can ever fully utter forth the infinite within it, in human speech. In prayer only do we seem to rise to that divine extasia when our souls mingle and blend with the one universal soul of the Universe, and, therefore, with truth, one of the Platonists has divinely called prayer φυγη μονου προς μονον—the flight of the Alone to the Alone.

The full emancipation of the spirit, the rending of the bondage which fetters and limits it here within a prison, will be the work of an eternity. It takes millions of years to perfect a

world ; it may take millions on millions to perfect a human soul; and as here on earth each
generation hands on the torch of light to the
next, and we walk in the accumulated light of
all the ages—so the soul will gather light in its
progress from star to star, for ever ascending
nearer the throne, but never one with God.
Thus the individuality of each conscious being
is preserved, and God and the soul remain
eternally distinct though eternally united, in the
same relation as the planet worlds to the central
sun.

In contemplating the solar system in its unity,
one is struck with the singularly rhythmic arrangement which connects planet with planet in
one harmonious chord. Pythagoras compared
the solar system to the chords of a lute, and had
we ears to hear, what a magnificent diapason
would reach us from the highest to the lowest
note of their grand choral music, as the planets
rush through space in orbits of well-adjusted
harmonic distances! The relation to the number three is particularly worthy of note; the
ancients have noticed this *Triad* in all things.
Taking, for example, the inner planets, we find
the year of Mercury to be about three months ;
Venus, six months ; the Earth, twelve months ;
and Mars, twenty-four months.

Then, also, in their respective distances from the sun, the same relation to the number three is observable. In approximate figures, Mercury is distant thirty millions of miles ; Venus, sixty; the Earth, ninety ; and Mars, one hundred and eighty millions of miles from the sun.

After passing these four smaller planets a great break occurs in the order of the system. In place of one large planet there are numerous fragments, like islands in an æther ocean, either parts of a shattered world, or masses of material which never yet had the power to cohere, being drawn in opposite directions by the opposing influences of Jupiter and the Sun.

On passing from these half-formed worlds we arrive at a new order of planets of immense magnitude and immense length of years, but with days only half the length of ours. The four inner planets have a day of twenty-four hours ; the four outer and larger a day of only nine hours or a little more.

The relation to the number three is also manifest in the stupendous masses of the outer planets.

Jupiter, the first and largest, thirteen hundred times greater than the earth, has a year, or period of rotation round the sun, of twelve of our years ; Saturn, next in order, of thirty years ;

Uranus of ninety years ; and Neptune, the last
and outermost, of one hundred and sixty years.
It is distant from the sun three thousand millions
of miles, and the pale satellite that has been
discovered attending its path has a solar distance
of three times three thousand millions of miles.
So that from the first planet, with its year of
three months, and solar distance of thirty
millions of miles, to the last revolving in the
outer darkness, the relation to the number three
still holds its remarkable place.

There may be some mystic symbolism in
these numbers, for all Nature is full of symbol-
isms, if we could only find the key.   And in
these immense orbs and orbits there is no
vagueness, no element of chance ; all is ordained
with the precision of a mathematical intelligence
and designer.

With regard to the duration of life in the
other planets, one cannot avoid hazarding
some curious speculations   If the inhabitants,
like man, are given about three score revolutions round the sun as the period of an ordinary
life, then, in Jupiter, the natural life would be
seven hundred years ; in Saturn, a thousand
years ; in Uranus, five thousand years ; and
in Neptune life would reach to the enormous
extent of ten thousand years.

It is, indeed, impossible to believe that in those outer planets, with their immense orbits, the length of life would only equal ours ; for, if so, those born in spring, in Neptune, for instance, would never gather the autumn fruits, and those born in winter would never see the summer flowers.

Yet, we have every reason to think that as there exists in these worlds a succession of seasons, and of day and night, so there must be seed time and harvest ; the necessity of sustenance, of toil to produce it, and of rest when the work is done.   In fact, that the lives of rational beings throughout all the worlds must be of the nature of the human, and, therefore, the duration of life must be in proportion to the sequence of the seasons.   And from this enormous length of life they probably attain to a height of power and knowledge impossible to man in the brief span of threescore years. For the human intellect is limited in its operations chiefly because of the frail and rapidly decaying mechanism with which it is united, and through which alone it can manifest itself.

What wonders might be achieved in Art and Science if only man were given a more powerful organisation, and a few centuries more of life.

In the larger planets the material frames are, no doubt, proportionate to the vast length of life in strength and vitality, and are thus enabled to resist the disintegrating action of forces which destroy human organisations in the poor limit of seventy years—a period which does not even equal six months of life in the planet Neptune.

But in the minor planets, where the annual revolution is so brief, the conditions of life must be singularly different. The year of Mercury is but a summer's day, and that of Venus little more. Yet there also we find the regularly recurring seasons and the alternating day and night, as if toil and rest were as necessary as upon earth. But in those fiery regions can there be toil? or do souls pass swiftly through them as through a purifying fire, before entering the temple of the sun, there to rest for ever-more, after their long wanderings of expiation through the series of the outer worlds ? Perfect happiness may, indeed, never be experienced in any grade of being ; there will still be pain— not the pain resulting from weak organisations, such as ours, but the pain of unfulfilled aspir-ations, of unsatisfied desires—the finite still seeking to grasp the infinite, and finding still an infinite beyond. In such pain, however, there is no misery, rather, as Schopenhaur has remarked, the intensest consciousness of life. Without it, life would be mere passivity—a dull negation, where the upward striving of the soul would be annihilated.

But the *Weltschmerz*—that nameless, bitter despair which haunts humanity—may have no place in a life that finds power always ready to equal aspiration. The triumphs of intellect will be more splendid, and the soul devoted to the culture of the beautiful will then be able to manifest the ideal in more perfect symbols.

The recognition of truth, and the power to give it form in word or act, will always be the chief joy of exalted natures, even as it is here on earth to those who value the spiritual above the sensual life. But here we only see as in a glass darkly; those who attain the higher life will read the mysteries of the universe by a purer light. Yet ascension may not be the immediate destiny of all. Those who voluntarily debase their nature to the level of the animal may be further debased for a time, and degraded to an existence fitted for lower brute natures, until, after the lapse of ages, elevation becomes possible, through the expiation of sorrow; while those who have led the divine life on earth—the life after the spirit, and not after the flesh—will rise at once to diviner heights of being in higher and nobler worlds.

The ancient philosophers, from Pythagoras to Plato, and from Plato to Plotinus, have uttered many beautiful and striking thoughts concerning the state of the soul after death. Especially are the Neo-Platonists full of divine utterances, though they, indeed, may have caught the inspiration from St Paul, with whose opinions, particularly as expressed in that marvellous masterpiece of eloquence, the 15th of 1st Corinthians, their writings on a similar subject have a remarkable affinity. As St Paul himself, a man of learning and genius, was not uninfluenced by the writings of Plato and Aristotle, with whose works he must have been perfectly familiar, having been brought up, as he expresses it, at the feet of Gamaliel, the most learned Jew of the period, and remarkable for his love of the Greek writers and his endeavours to introduce the knowledge of Greek literature and philosophy amongst the Jewish youth.

It is singular that, with all the mechanical aids now given to science, the moderns, so far as the knowledge of a future life is concerned, have not passed the level reached by the sublime guesses of the ancients. The philosophers of above two thousand years ago recognised and affirmed progressive mutation under immutable laws ; the incessant destruction and renovation of all things ; the dual nature of man, half animal, half God ; the opposing forces of attraction and repulsion, of love and hate, as the principle of motion in all things ; the necessity of the knowledge of evil, through which alone the soul learns to know its strength ; the origin of all things from fire, which is the theory of Mr Proctor, as well as of Empedocles, and the purification of the soul through infinite progression and ascension, as taught by Plato.

Plato asserts that our souls, ' when they are perfectly established with the Soul of the World, will be likewise perfect, reign on high, and govern the universe itself.' And souls of this exalted nature will be shrined in a glorified form, subject neither to infirmity nor defect. And Plotinus maintains that ' souls are eternally changing forms ; and as often as a soul is able to rise beyond the bounds of earthly generation, it lives divinely with the universal soul.'

The theory of the existence of another life necessarily means a higher life—for we judge by analogy—all things here rise to a higher life through death, by which they attain to a nobler incarnation.

The sublime views of Plato on the descent of

the soul into the body, as into a prison house, or sepulchre, having first drank of the waters of oblivion before entering the earthly life, and its subsequent resurrection and purification through death, find credence in many thoughtful minds, though visible, tangible proof may be wanting of the truth of the theory. We moderns come, perhaps, too arrogantly and proudly into the temple of knowledge. We stand when we should kneel; and irony and self-sufficing dogmatism discard with a sarcasm all belief in mysteries which cannot be verified by experience and observation. The final word of the modern philosophy is, that we know nothing of life beyond the grave, because nothing can be known. But the soul refuses to accept this final word, and still searches the infinite for some symbol, or analogy, or law that can give the hope of a future life redeemed from the narrow limitations of the present, and confirm the prescience of an existence transfigured to glory by unclouded intellect, a finer organism, and the highest aims of a purified moral nature.

With this hope we can better sustain the mysterious dispensation of sorrow that shrouds this earthly life, and the coming of that awful moment of gloom when death lays on us his icy hand to draw us down to the grave,—

Nor think it misery to be a man ;
Who thinks it is will never be a God.

If it be impossible to prove the unknown and
the unknowable, it is equally impossible to era-
dicate the universal intuition of humanity that
the soul will one day be emancipated from the
prison house, and arise from the sepulchre.
Faber, the great religious poet of the century,
has expressed this yearning of the soul towards
freedom in verse as beautiful as Plato's words:—

We have imprisoned by our sin
Man's dread intelligences,
And broken lights are flooded in
Upon them by the senses.
She sitteth there, a captive maiden,
Upon the cold bars leaning,
Until her bosom is dread-laden,
With all Life's lustrous meaning.

Of all the Arts by which the Invisible, the
Ideal and the Eternal are manifested, perhaps music excels all others in its power to
reveal to us the existence of this dimly discovered higher life of the future ; and there are
moments when, lifted to ecstasy by the inspiration of music, we feel the deep affinity of the
human with the divine intelligence, and a belief
in the invisible comes over the mind with the
strength of the proto-martyr's faith when, looking upward with death-shadowed eyes, he saw

Heaven opened, and Christ, the head and type of a glorified humanity, standing at the right hand of God.

The followers of Pythagoras made a beautiful use of music as an influence to act upon the spiritual nature.   Before retiring to rest they purified the reason by certain odes and peculiar songs which quieted the perturbations of the day ; and sometimes even by musical sounds alone they healed the passions of the soul as if by enchantment.

And it was their idea that the soul, before she gave herself up to the body, was the auditor of divine harmony, and that now some melodies heard on earth have the power to wake within her the memory of that music, and she is lifted by it into a divine sympathy with the divine.

The greatest names in the world's intellectual history have upheld the theory that our earth is not the sole point in the infinite cosmic scheme where conscious intelligence exists.   Indeed, so instinctive is the belief in life in other worlds, that the doctrine is accepted by most minds passively, and without examining the grounds upon which belief may be based.   Mr Proctor, though he does not write to prove that there are other inhabited worlds, yet is led up to the con-viction by his own deductions from physical phenomena. His views, however, though eminent for the brilliancy and power with which they are set forth, and made comprehensible to all, even the most unscientific minds, differ in no way from those expressed by Kant a century ago in his work, entitled *A General History aud Theory of the Heavens.* Both he and Mr Proctor hold the belief in the succession of vital epochs; in the luminosity of Jupiter as a life-giving sun; and the incessant formation and destruction of worlds by absorption into their primaries, from whence they are again cast forth by the action of heat, to commence anew their existence as revolving systems round a central sun.

The views of the great German philosopher concerning the inhabitants of the planets are worthy of note. He affirms his belief that the perfection of spiritual and material life in the planet worlds increases in direct proportion to their distance from the sun. Thus Mercury and Venus are placed in the lowest degree of existence; the earth holds an average place—imperfect still, but showing signs of progression, while the highest development is found in the outer regions of the solar system. And he assigns as a reason that the density of the larger planets is much less, and the materials of which they are formed are much less coarse and ponderous than those of the inner planets, which we are accustomed to consider as the bright and beautiful regions of eternal summer.

In studying these theories of the Infinite Cosmos, an involuntary shudder of awe, almost of terror, comes over the mind at the thought that we, frail, weak, much-suffering mortals, evolved from matter by the eternal forces, why or how we know not, without our volition, without the power to fall out of the ranks into the rest of annihilation, are destined for ever and for ever to endless mutations of form in an endless succession of lives, still, perhaps, of toil and labour and sorrow, under an eternal and change-less system of inflexible law. Turn where we will, the despotism of law confronts us. There is no escape from this awful all-compelling power. Sentient or non-sentient, the monads of the universe must exist throughout all eternity, and fulfil the work destined for them by the unseen Omnipotent Intelligence, who reveals himself only through laws. And each day, as science extends her conquests over ignorance, more and more of the phenomena of life and the universe are placed under law.

We now know that all evil, all crime and vice, with their consequences of social and moral ruin, all disasters and catastrophes by which thousands perish, and all the ills that flesh is heir to, result from the violation or disregard of some law, physical or moral. Yet, granting this, we stand before the thick darkness of another mystery. Happiness, as might naturally be expected, does not in this world follow obedience to law—at least, as far as regards the outer life. 'The wicked flourish like a green bay tree; the righteous perish and no man layeth it to heart.' The recompense and the punishment, then, must be *within*. There is, probably, no suffering like remorse, no peace like that of a good conscience, void of offence before God and men. The compensation will come, perhaps, in those higher states of being in which we all must believe. Suffering in our mortal life would be unjust unless it were meant for purification, because it would be useless. The idea that lies at the basis of all things in the universe is ultimate good, a man must work out this idea in the world which he has been given to rule, through obedience to laws written on his heart, revealed in nature, and manifested through the history of all human lives.

Perfect obedience to the divine idea may never be attained. God alone *is ;* man is eternally *becoming*. But through the endless succession of ages and of existences, each diviner than the preceding, the soul will go on unto perfection, until the physical and moral nature attain to their full beauty and harmony, and men shall be as gods.

Mr Proctor deserves the thanks of the age for having given a fresh stimulus to this most important subject by his learned and lucid works. The bold and brilliant audacity with which he unveils the mysteries of the infinite, his clear and eloquent, yet simple style, his vast generalisations and fearless assumptions from the known to the unknown, combine to make his astronomical essays the most exciting and profoundly interesting of all the speculative studies recently given to literature. His facts and deductions are alike dazzling, from the wide amplitude and universal range of his knowledge over all that exists ; and though he reasons entirely from physical phenomena, as they have been, are now, and will be in the eternal duration and eternal change of all things, yet he, as well as Mr Hamilton, whose arguments presuppose a religious belief, can recognise the signature of the Omnipotent God written upon the mighty dome of Heaven in heiroglyphics, whose glorious symbols are worlds and suns and systems re-volving throughout eternity.

O

AUSTRALIA.

(*A Plea for Emigration.*)

MR FOSTER FITZGERALD, late Colonial Secretary at Victoria, in his excellent history of Australia, contributed to the series entitled *Foreign Countries and British Colonies*, sets one's mind seriously thinking on the great question of Emigration.

No subject, indeed, can be of higher importance to our weary and dispirited generation than the condition and resources of the vast southern continent that forms so magnificent a portion of England's colonial empire. Statesmen and politicians are beginning at last to recognise the truth that to colonise a new country is the one great remedial measure for the suffering classes of the Old World ; for all who in our overcrowded cities and professions and trades are ever vainly seeking and hopelessly awaiting the employment that never comes, the income that never is realised.

Whoever, then, can aid the youth of the
empire to leave the old grooves and seek new
fields of enterprise is a benefactor to the age.
And Mr Fitzgerald's work affords exactly the
information most necessary to the colonist.
Full details are given of the climate, the soil,
the various sources of wealth, with the peculiar
laws and social elements of each Australian
province; so the adventurous settler can at
once judge for himself what locality is best
suited to his habits and pursuits, his consti-
tution and his temperament.

Maps and copious statistics are also included
in the work, which brings down the history of
the colonies to the present time, and leaves no
point of importance untouched.

The splendid picture drawn by the ex-secre-
tary of the wealth, energy and progress of this
new world, makes one feel still more vividly the
helpless destitution and misery of the millions
at home, and the importance of arousing men's
minds to the great fact that this vast Australian
continent belongs to no alien race, but is the
heritage of our own people, won from chaos by
their energy and daring, part of our own empire,
with the same sympathies and interests, and
every subject of the realm can enter in through
its wide-open portals and share its wealth, and

profit by its infinite resources, without let or
hindrance. It is but a narrow view to limit a
man's rights to the little island or parish where
he may have been born. The whole earth has
been given to the children of men, and they
should go forth boldly and claim their birthright. The migration of nations is a fiat of
Providence. It has been going on with the
regularity of a law for six thousand years, and
to our great Japetian race, the highest of
humanity, seems especially to have been given
the strength, the will, the intellect, and the
power to make the circuit of the globe, going
forth conquering and to conquer, with a mission
to rule and lead wherever they lift their flag and
plant their foot within the wide circuit of the
world.

The eternal march of civilisation knows
neither pause nor rest. It sweeps like destiny
over the desolate unsouled lands where nature
has lain torpid since creation ; and over the
rude, half-souled savage tribes of the earth.
And no people should debar themselves from
the privilege of joining the ranks of progress ;
for there are endless sources of wealth still
unutilised ; vast tracks still untrodden, waiting
the transforming energy of intellect and science
to make the wilderness blossom as a rose.

Why, then, should not the vital force of our people be employed on these lines of certain profit, in place of being wasted year by year in the bitter strife with other men as destitute as themselves, for an acre of land more or less in the old country, some wild tract of dreary bog, or a few stacks of turf on some desolate moor, while all the time a new world is waiting to be occupied, where everything they had dreamed of vainly, and worked for sadly from their youth up can be realised and enjoyed. Every day the strife for bread here is growing more fierce, the struggle more desperate for the smallest gain, and the misery and want still deeper and darker; so one cannot wonder if the suffering masses, ground down as they are by taxation, trodden down by the rush of the crowd, crushed by reckless competition, and galled and tortured by the impassable barrier between the Haves and the Wants, should be driven to revolution by despair.

Life at present, even in industrious England, is a bitter heritage to many—a scroll written within and without with lamentations and mourning and woe. There is a feverish strain in all departments of the social system, an unhealthy excitement, everyone seeking the means to live with terrible eagerness, and few finding any adequate result. Crowds working like convicts on the daily treadmill, joyless and hopeless, till they drop from exhaustion into the grave ; others, strong and stalwart men, standing idle in the market-place because no one has hired them ; while the young and brilliant rush desperately into literature, that last resource of the unfortunate, and write novels, which they publish, probably at their own expense, or fling themselves body and soul to the devouring hydra of journalism, to live and work and die without recognition or honour, distinction or reward.

Life, in fact, has become a mean and ignoble scramble for the mere means of living. And all sensitive natures behold with dismay and terror the vile servitude of the intellect to the baser needs of life, and the degradation of the noblest instincts of the soul which the strife for money entails ; when a man dare not swerve one inch from the narrow groove prescribed by party politics, or our old social conventions, lest he should loose his chance of bread and be no longer hired to sweep the floor of civilisation for the shreds and fragments society may have let fall by the way—that one department of intellectual activity which now seems the most popular and the best paid.

The great high priest of Pessimism, Arthur
Schopenhauer, felt so keenly the discord and
misery of life that he expressed his surprise the
whole human race did not some day resolve to
make an end of it by a simultaneous and com
prehensive suicide; so, looking at the object
struggles with poverty of the millions in these
British Isles, one wonders they do not arrange
amongst themselves for a general stampede into
the German Ocean on the one hand and the
Atlantic on the other. But, happily, the burden
of existence can be lightened without resorting
to the extreme measures advocated by the
Pessimist philosophy. A sail across the ocean
might be tried before a final plunge into its
depth; and perhaps an intelligent study of the
advantages of Australian colonisation would
even persuade the despairing bread-seekers at
home to give life another chance at the anti-
podes. For what has our political and social
system come to in this effete Europe? Mr
Ruskin describes the result in his strong eloquent phrases: 'The evidences of it are degraded art, mean pleasures, merciless war, sullen
toil; the glory of it emaciated with cruel hunger
and blotted with venomous stain, and the trail
of it a glittering slime.' Surely then, there can
be nothing cruel in asking these victims of

hunger and want, of degradation and vain hope, to turn their eyes to the great land where there is work and wealth for everyone; no war, no want, no hunger; and no fear of overcrowding in a continent as large almost as all Europe, yet with a population only equal to half that of London.

It is remarkable, also, that just as the old countries begin to fail in resources, and men eagerly search for new and wider spheres of action along with the freedom and adventure of an untried life, the veil is suddenly lifted from some hitherto unknown region, and a new heritage is given to humanity.   Plain and river and forest and mine are made to yield up their treasures, and science and industry win new victories over ignorance and barbarism.   Thus America was revealed to civilisation in order that commerce and intellect might replace the buffalo and the savage on the wild prairies of the West.   And when America was lost to England another field of action was found for the enterprise of the nation in the *terra australis incognita* of the Southern Sea.

The Dutch, in their wanderings from the Spice Islands of the Indian Archipelago, had come on this vast continent lying on the borders of the Pacific, but England only began to found settlements on the east coast about a century ago. No one then imagined that the land was paved with gold. It was used merely as a waste dust-heap for the refuse population of the empire, while but few independent settlers were found brave enough to dare the dangers of its untried desolation.

From a beginning so unpromising the Australian nation has arisen, industrious, wealthy and self-governed ; splendid in enterprise and in all modes of material and intellectual progress. Magnificent cities have sprung up where but a few years ago the New Holland savage hunted the kangaroo ; a fine export trade has been established, and limitless vistas of wealth have been opened to the colonist in a country that by its position commands the trade with India, China, Japan and America, along with the islands of the Southern Sea.

Sydney was the first great settlement, selected for its harbour, where the navy of a world might anchor. Being the oldest colony, the Sydney people consider themselves the Aristos, the true noble class. They retain much of the fair English beauty that marks their origin, with also much of the stately forms of English society, and in splendour and pleasure Sydney almost rivals London. But Sydney soon became overcrowded and expensive, land rose to a fabulous price, and so new colonists went forth and built other cities—Adelaide, superb in climate and scenery; and Melbourne, the Athens of the State, where the highest culture is honoured and art and beauty have their temples. The fine library there to which all classes are admissible, built at a cost of two hundred and eighty thousand pounds, is one of the finest buildings in the world; and a National Gallery has been founded to contain replicas of all the great pictures of Europe, selected by Mr Ruskin and other eminent critics, with casts of the most famous statues, ancient and modern.

Melbourne is wealthy, and can afford these costly accessories of life. Since the auriferous fields were discovered, only fifty years ago, gold to the value of one hundred and ninety-two millions has been obtained, and the average annual return of gold is six millions. Ten thousand steam engines are ever at work on the quartz reefs, while still the yield seems inexhaustible. And this is but a fragment of the great gold land, whose full extent no man knows as yet.

Railroads traverse the States in every direction, and one has been already projected to span the whole Continent from south to north, at a cost of ten millions sterling ; while a telegraphic line, two thousand miles long, brings it into immediate communication with the whole world.

There are millions of acres growing the finest wheat ; plains of pasturage for cattle that would feed the whole empire ; riches in coal and all the useful metals as yet only partly explored ; while the great mountain wall that guards the coast from the Pacific seems based upon a pediment of gold. In one year twelve millions of gold were realised by Victoria alone, and it has been computed that since the discovery of the gold-fields two hundred and sixty millions sterling in gold have been added by Australia to the wealth of the world.

But the gold fever has already cooled down, now that the alluvial deposits are almost exhausted, for working by machinery on the quartz reefs is too costly for the ordinary gold-digger. Gold nuggets, worth many thousands, can no longer be picked up in a morning's walk, but men have found a truer and more profitable source of wealth in the cultivation of the soil, and in all those natural resources fitted to sustain life, of which, indeed, gold is but the accepted symbol. The real inexhaustible wealth of Australia is in agriculture, and the stream of emigration may still go on, and find ample space and verge enough.

Western Australia is still almost untenanted. These endless plains of the West and the interior, sombre, silent and gloomy, that fill the beholder with a sense of oppressive desolation, wait the tranforming energy of our race to give them a soul, and bring them within the circle of living humanity.

England now expends above one hundred and thirty millions sterling for imported food. When these waste plains are cultivated, Australia can supply it all, and give the millions of her gold in return for English manufactures. Already she pays about seventeen millions a year for English goods. Thus the two countries can be mutually useful, the only fitting relation between the various portions of the empire, and the only one that can insure the loyalty of the colonies and dependencies to the Crown. Australia is loyal because it is her interest to be so. The bond is one of mutual advantage, not of subjection and tyranny. England appoints the governors to each province, but this is the only mark of sovereignty she is permitted to assume.

Australia is perfectly free of all external control, and is entirely self-governed, the result being that although civilisation there is scarcely

a century old, yet the States already rival
Europe in magnificence, while they far excel
the old nations of the world in the human
progress which consists in the well-being, the
prosperity, comfort, freedom and sense of personal dignity of every member of the community. A few resolute men, unfettered by
cant, prejudice or routine, have achieved there
in a few years the almost perfect form of a
free Government, after which Europe has been
blindly groping for a thousand years through
much blood and many revolutions, with all
their adjuncts of scaffolds and martyrdoms, but
has never yet reached or realised.

Each state has its independent legislature,
makes its own laws, and controls its own taxation and finance. There are some minor
differences, but all agree in giving to man the
full charter of his rights. The leading principles
are the same in all—manhood suffrage, liberal
land laws, extended secular education, no state
church, free libraries, splendid universities where
women are eligible for degrees as well as men,
triennial parliaments, an elective Upper House,
no rights of primogeniture, no privileged class
with traditions of superior wisdom and divine
right of rule attached to the accident of birth,
but each man takes rank according to his worth

and work. Society is thoroughly democratic, all are workers, and all are equal. A career is open to every man with the certainty of reward, and in the fullest sense the land is for the people.

Australia has thus solved quietly and peaceably the problem which in Europe has set Communist, Socialist and Nihilist at war with all existing governments. Vainly, however, they rave and rage, and slay and die; the stifling traditions of the Old World social system still exist; and the problem still remains unsolved in Europe. But in Australia the colossal experiment has been tried and has succeeded, to found a nation on the broad principles of freedom and justice with the widest recognition of human rights, and a great, powerful and progressive people has been the result; free as America, self-reliant as England, strong as ancient Rome under the Republic, though no standing army is required to uphold its power.

Why, then, do not trades' unions and mechanics' institutes and popular lecturers, and workmen's clubs, take up this subject of colonisation, and show the intelligent youth of the country the advantages offered by this new world of vitality and progress over the decadence and stagnation of exhausted Europe ?

And why, above all, should the force and fire of Irish manhood be wasted in vain complaints that their people are ' the worst fed, the worst housed, the worst clothed, the most utterly destitute of any of the nations of the earth ' (which indeed is a sad truth), when they could arise and go forth to a noble and splendid heritage ? No tenant is forced to remain on the land in Ireland. He is perfectly free to leave if he considers himself rack-rented. And, at the same time, the landlord is quite justified in letting his land for the highest price that will be given. Many will give fancy prices for property on account of the scenery, the picturesque view, from old associations, or for convenience of locality ; and a landlord has as much right to sell his land to the best advantage as a Manchester cotton merchant to sell his goods at the highest profit.

Irish poverty is in truth the melancholy but logical result of centuries of misgovernment, begun originally in spoliation and continued in apathy and indifference to the welfare of the people, varied with spasmodic intervals of vehement coercion and abrogation of all legal rights ; while all the time the great material resources of the country were left entirely undeveloped—the land, the fisheries, the mines,

the marble quarries, the vast water-power, the
splendid lakes and harbours, with the means
of rapid transit by railways—all were miser-
ably neglected ; as a proof of which may be
mentioned that for years the people of the
west have been desirous of a railroad from
Galway to Cong, a distance only of thirty miles,
but it has never been accomplished.   A steamer
plies in summer on Lough Corrib between
the two places, but ceases in winter ; so through
all this inclement season the poor peasants are
obliged to trudge backward and forward *on
foot* with their market produce, between the
capital of the west and the small county towns.
Yet, in the same space of time, the Americans
have completed ninety thousand miles of working railways radiating all over their continent,
a result that proves the advantage of a local
government with a knowledge of the land
and an interest in the people, over government
by a distant legislature without the requisite
knowledge, or the natural interest and loving
bond of kinship.

   No individuals out of their own private means,
still less Irish landlords, can undertake national
works on any broad and extensive scale.   They
must be organised by the government of the
country, and paid for out of the national ex-

chequer. This has been done in Australia. In New South Wales, for instance, the Government has spent nine millions sterling on railroads, three hundred thousand on harbours, and similar sums on public roads and buildings. It is by such means that the intellect and the energies of a people are aroused, and wealth, peace, happiness and prosperity are assured.

Ireland has never yet been favoured with beneficial legislation of the kind, and now the Government seems inclined, as a final resource of civilisation, to annihilate the gentry in order that the peasants may live ; there not being room enough in Ireland, apparently, for both classes to exist together on the land. And supposing this desired result obtained, that the prisons were filled with the youth and intelligence of the country, the landlords ruined, and the peasants set in their place, how will the condition of the nation be advanced by the robbery of one class to feed another? One shudders to think of Ireland mapped out into five million of potato plots, each fenced by its rude stone wall ; the beautiful and the picturesque utterly sacrificed without even wealth being gained, for all progress will be rendered impossible. Progress requires capital and culture, science and knowledge ; and these true

P

'resources of civilisation' could scarcely be found in a flourishing state amongst five million of peasants, each on his one-acre holding— a mere nation of labourers degenerating to paupers, while the land would gradually retrograde to primeval bog.

In Australia, on the contrary, there is room for all classes and many Irelands, and no one need stand on the dead to clutch at rent-rolls.

The poor Irish settler who now treads his dreary round of life in the furrows of his scanty potato-field would there find tracts of the finest land—twenty, thirty, forty thousand acre farms to be had for a mere nominal price—while all the political dreams would be actually realised that in Ireland seem now but the vain hope of despairing men ; land without the incubus of a landlord ; a true Republic though under the flag of monarchy ; work and wages for everyone ; and a powerful and important Irish party, who have already created a new Ireland in the southern sea, strong, wealthy and independent, yet with the love for the old country still unchanged, as was shown by their munificent contribution of sixty thousand pounds to the suffering Irish during the famine years.

At present about a hundred thousand emi-

grants leave Ireland yearly for America; but
Australia would be a better and wider field for
enterprise, and, as part of our own empire, ought
to have special advantages for the colonist.
There is not much roughing to be feared; the
climate is excellent, and yields readily every
esculent known to Europe along with those
peculiar to the tropics; while all the new aids
to life which science has discovered will be found
in full working order; for Australia has had no
long ignorant childhood like the other nations
of the earth, but is the heir of all the ages, and
entered at once into the nineteenth century
inheritance of civilisation, so has been able to
utilise every modern idea by her exhaustless resources and untrammelled energy. The voyage
that used to take eight months to accomplish,
and was entered on with the dread of eternal
banishment, is now but a pleasure trip of forty
days; the climate all along the coast is perfect
and peculiarly suited to the Irish, who cannot
well endure the rigours of a Canadian winter;
while the pastoral and agricultural employments
exactly suit the Irish temperament and habits.
No wars are possible, no hostile tribes are to be
feared, for the Aborigines have nearly become
extinct; there are no fierce beasts of prey, and
but little of the still fiercer elements of a de-

graded humanity, for the convict sediment that formed the earliest social stratum has long since been covered and obliterated by the waves of advancing civilisation.

Tasmania, once in reality the home of demons, is now a garden of loveliness, as large as all England, and with all the refinements of English life.   Norfolk Island is a paradise of beauty, the air divine, the scenery fine and romantic.   Melbourne has the softness of Southern Italy and Sydney glows with the radiance of the Grecian Isles.   The death-rate is low in all these favoured portions of the States, far lower than the English average.   And the English race does not deteriorate, but the children grow up tall, fair and handsome, while the nerve power and energy for daring and enterprise seem even heightened.

Victoria, with its rich soil, splendid climate, and glittering streams, sands, and rocks of gold, has become the queen of the Australian States, though but a barren wilderness fifty years ago. The gold madness raged there fiercely for a brief space, and life became an inferno, and the land was accursed through crime ; but all that has passed away, and the gold quest proceeds now with admirable order under Government control.

Besides, the colonists have found that the

honest toil of agriculture is safer and better in the end than the rude, reckless life and wild chances of the gold diggers. Immense fortunes are still realised by gold speculations, but more easily and certainly by the growth of wheat and the rearing of cattle for the manufacturing millions of England.

The Irish can well estimate the advantages of emigration by comparing the condition of their countrymen now in America with those left at home chafing in discontent, reckless, hopeless, miserable, without any stimulus to work or means of advancement.

The American Irish are now a great and powerful nation of ten millions, with wealth in abundance, as is proved by the fact that they could send over two thousand a week to Ireland as a contribution to aid what they considered the national cause. Had their fathers remained at home the children would now be only miserable cottiers like the rest of their kindred, with no profit, after the rent was paid, beyond what would give them a daily dinner of potatoes, and meat, perhaps, once a year. And there are now forty thousand of these cottiers in Ireland living on less than an acre of land each.

The Australian Irish will in time be as powerful a people as their American kindred, and the

chances of wealth are even greater in Australia
with its population of two millions only, than
in America with its sixty millions. The emigrant will find in Australia farms as large as
all Ireland to be had for a shilling an acre,
and he could raise thousands of pounds from
his sheep-walk in less time than he now expends
in fighting desperately with his impoverished
landlord for the reduction of a few shillings an
acre at home, which reduction, even if obtained,
brings in nothing to the wealth of the country.
It is merely a case of money changing hands
amongst the classes of the same community.
Besides, when the Australian Irish have amassed
sufficient funds they can return to Green Erin
and buy up the estates of the pauperised landlords, who will then only be too happy to obtain
any chance of sale for their profitless acres.

Considering the destitution of millions of the
working classes, and even of the educated and
cultured in these British Islands, it is surprising
that the subject of emigration to the great rich
lands of other portions of the Empire has not
been taken up seriously and energetically by
the nation and the Government as the one great
measure of national salvation.

Out of the five millions of Ireland, a million
or two of the young generation might well be

spared for the chances of a nobler life in the
New World. The remainder would then have
room and land enough to enjoy life at home,
and even add to homely comforts some of the
luxury and beauty which give a moral refinement to a people.

Every cottage might then have its garden and
pleasure-ground for the young children, every
village its people's park, and every household
the order, neatness and purity of Christian
civilisation.

The world is large enough and rich enough
to allow every man free space and pure air.
But we absurdly insist on crowding people
together in one small locality, as if it were a
praiseworthy thing, and a proof of the prosperity of a country, to have as many human
beings as possible to every square rood of
ground ; whereas a dense population is invari-
ably, and of necessity, a dense mass of poverty,
and too often of sin, and a mournful effort to
live without any of the joy of living. At present no class in Ireland is content, for no one
seems to have any assured income. The gentry
want money, and the peasants want land without paying rent for it, and strive to obtain it by
means not quite satisfactory to the owners, such
as burnings and slaughter and general devasta-

tion—a mode of regenerating a country happily not needed in the great Australian land.

The State, also, would be a gainer if the few were left to peace and comfort, while the many were relieved from want by emigration.

Fifty thousand soldiers were recently required in our little island, only a hundred miles broad, to guard the granaries of the rich from the thin hands of the poor; and every potato was watched by a policeman, and every turnip by a dragoon, and no pig could go to market without an escort of cavalry; and the prisons were filled with hundreds of young men who were eating the bread of compulsory idleness at the expense of the taxpayers, while they could have been of immense use and value, if only tending sheep and growing corn for the Empire on the broad plains of the southern continent.

There the colonists could have a wilderness of land for the asking; pastures for flocks and herds, were they numerous as the leaves of the forest trees; and no standing army is required to guard the potatoes and turnips, but every man is able and willing to defend his own rights and the rights of others, for there is no antagonism between the State and the people; all work harmoniously together for the general good. Even the effort to introduce manufactures into

Ireland offers but a poor equivalent for the certain advantage of Australian enterprise. And, in fact, the idea of making Ireland a manufacturing country is a delusion to be avoided.

Nature has given her rich plains for pasturage, a splendid seaboard for fisheries, and the charms of wild and beautiful scenery, but has denied the elements of manufacturing success. England has coal and iron, a powerful army to force the opening of new marts of commerce, a powerful mercantile navy to aid and guard her merchants, and a thousand years' practice in trade. Ireland has none of these things, and all competition with England for manufactures simply means wasted effort and deplorable failure, and would be as absurd as competition with France for silk, or with China for tea.

Every part of the Empire has its peculiar province ; that of England is to provide cutlery and calico. This suits the hard, stolid, industrious Saxon, who never lifts his eyes from the toil of his hands, and has no need to lift them, for he has no ideal and no aspirations beyond food and wages. But the Irish are quite unsuited to the rigid bondage of manufacturing work, and would be altogether miserable in the dark, depressing, prisoned factory life. They need the sunlight and the open air, where the

laughter of children can be heard ; their light,
joyous temperament requires constant diversity,
with frequent rest for social talk, and the sense
of individual freedom in the broad rich fields
and healthful air. Therefore the pastoral and
agricultural life was specially designed for them
by Providence, not the crowded dens of factory
toil with the drone of the wheels for ever in
their ears. They have the linen manufacture
already, founded by the French and worked
chiefly by Scotch factory hands ; and they have
the poplin manufacture, also founded by the
French ; these have achieved success and may
safely be continued. But the trades of the forge
and the furnace should be left to England, as
we leave dolls to Nuremberg, and watches to
Geneva, and silks to Lyons.

And what can be more bright and joyous or
better suited to the Irish nature than the golden
vales and emerald plains of their fair country
covered with flocks and herds, or the silver
salmon leaping in the nets, under the shadow
of the purple mountains of the West, where the
fiords of the Atlantic bite deep into the land,
and the rushing streamlets murmur a divine
music through the chasms of the hills.

Such a landscape never should be desecrated
by the tall chimneys of the factory prison, nor

by the smoke of the furnaces rising up to obscure heaven.

Ireland is a beautiful country, with its green
plains and wooded glens and the hundred
islands of the lakes, each made sacred by some
ancient cross or ruined oratory where a saint has
prayed. It is a land for the painter and poet,
for romance and legend and song ; for men to
hunt and fish and enjoy all manly sports in
festive freedom, and where the women grow up,
tall and beautiful in the pure air, with eyes deep
as their lakes and purple as their mountains ;
and in the soft Irish climate so little is required
for sustenance that a population of two or three
millions would find all they needed for enjoyment and even for luxury in the natural resources of the country, such as the pasturage
and the fisheries ; for these are the true riches of
Ireland, and if well worked and organised
would be found infinitely profitable, whereas a
competition with England in manufactures must
be ruinous if attempted, because so utterly
unsuited to the soil, the climate and the habits
and disposition of the Irish people.

Every nation has its mission ; that of England
is to be the great workshop of the world, to
supply man with everything he needs except
food.

Scotland builds ships and weaves and spins,
and supplies the leaders of Thought to the
Empire, as Carlyle and Ruskin, and others of
name and fame; while Ireland supplies the
mighty men of renown, the leaders of Action—
warriors, statesmen, orators, as Burke, Canning,
Wellington, Palmerston, and others down to the
present time ; and she is able besides to feed all
England with her flocks and all the world by
her fisheries. Let us then leave the Saxon
toilers, these true children of the mighty Thor,
to the din of the hammer and the whirl of the
wheels, but Ireland, *Innis Helga* (the Holy
Island), should be kept sacred to the picturesque,
a temple consecrated to nature where the weary
workers of the world might come to refresh
their arid souls by its lovely lakes and hills, and
drink in the pure ozone of the Atlantic breeze.

Yet to make Ireland attractive to tourists and
visitors from other lands, and so bring a stream
of wealth into the country, much progress is
required in the arts and appliances of civilisation
—good roads, good country hotels, pleasure
boats on the lakes, public gardens and parks,
branch railroads for safe and rapid transit, with
a line of passenger steamers to southern Europe.
It seems so absurd for the Irish now to have to
cross first to London if they wish to visit France

or Spain, when four or five hundred years ago
there was constant and direct communication
between Ireland and the Continent.   The Irish do
not seem to be fully and fearfully conscious how
infinitely they fall behind the other nations of
Europe in all that relates to the material well-
being of humanity.   They should be taught
discontent in place of patient calm and endur-
ance of their condition.   Discontent is the great
motive power of nations.   It is the knowledge
of the evil which must precede the remedy.   The
Irish peasants should learn that they are 'poor
and blind and naked,' that they live in hovels
and holes not fit for a dog, that their food is
poorer than that of the root-eating Indians, their
raiment the vilest of rags ; they should be made
to see that Ireland rests in the midst of progression 'like a frozen ship in a frozen sea,' and
that as regards the ordinary comforts and
common decencies of civilisation they are at
this moment lower than any Christian people
on the face of the earth, while if the natural
riches of the country were properly developed
by a local government and the resources of the
national exchequer, no people on the earth would
be happier or more prosperous than the Irish.

   But pending that good time let them take
possession of any other land that will give them

the food and raiment God meant for all men.
Let them fling up these miserable plots of poor,
exhausted ground, and go forth from their
wretched hovels to the bright, free country where
life is a joy and a blessing and work has its
reward, and wealth is certain to industry; for
in Australia the welfare of the people is the first
consideration, important before all others. The
improvement of the land is encouraged by cheap
law, low taxation, facility of purchase, with
merely nominal rent to the State; and all
measures that can promote the comfort, education, prosperity and enlightenment of the people
are organised by Government and accomplished
at an unlimited cost, and Ireland, if left but
with two or three millions of people to feed
and support, might attain also to that wealth
and happiness which is now impossible to a
nation of five millions of helpless paupers.

The land could be made a garden of beauty
by better cultivation, the people would find and
utilise the riches in the earth and sea so lavishly
given by nature. Visitors from all lands in
search of the picturesque would be welcomed
and honoured by the courteous and prosperous
peasants, and the world would not again have to
marvel at the want of gallantry that made Irishmen frighten away a charming Empress from

their shores, while they were waging a desperate and deadly struggle among themselves for bread.

But emigration is a great national measure, and should not be left to the slender resources of an impoverished people.

To be successful it must be organised by Government on a liberal and extensive scale, with bright prospects set before the youth of the country, and ample funds available for proper modes of transit to the new settlements.

A Minister of Emigration would be necessary to begin with; then an Emigrant Commission in Dublin, with branches throughout the country, at the head of which might be placed men of sense and knowledge, like Sir Charles Duffy and others, who have had long and intimate experience both of Australian and Irish life. There should be a line of emigrant ships, with free passage and proper comforts provided, free land given on arrival, without any rent for a certain number of years, after which a small tax might be paid to the State, but not to any intermediate landlord—the State alone should be the real guardian of all the land of a country; while emigrant homes should be provided under State supervision, where the colonists might be cared for until they found suitable employment. And every year a number of strong, intelligent children of both sexes should be selected from our parish and national schools, and trained for colonial life—the boys taught trades, the girls all the duties of a household ; and, when sufficiently educated, sent out under State control to the emigrant homes till they were properly located and settled.

Young men of a higher grade might be trained in an agricultural college and taught farming and engineering, for which there is always a great demand in a new country; and young ladies who passed the college course at home would find ready employment as teachers and professors in the colonies, where the universities have been thrown open to the competition of women equally with men.

Thus a happy and prosperous Irish nation would be created in Australia, while the nation at home might also become happy and prosperous if the redundant pauperised population of five millions were diminished to one-half, who might then live in peace and security.

But an extensive deportation from the over-crowded localities of the Empire need not be limited to Ireland. How much better and healthier would London be, for instance, if out of the five millions of its densely-packed population three millions were shipped off to the

wide plains of Australia or the invigorating
snows of Canada, and all the squalid streets
were cleared of the squalid life that now makes
them hideous and revolting to every sense.
These crowds of hunger - stricken, brutalised
men ; these stunted, ill-favoured women ; these
pallid, deformed children, where God's image
is defaced to ugliness by want of free space to
move in and fresh air to breathe—let them be
uprooted, in the common interests of humanity,
from the pestilence-stricken lanes and alleys
of the Great City, and transplanted to a free,
healthful soil, where the human form and the
immortal soul might grow in beauty under
kindlier influences.

Even amongst the higher classes a million or
so might well be spared from the crowd and
vain strife of London life. And what is there
to regret ? When Mr Mallock propounded the
question of the age, ' Is life worth living ? ' one
universal chorus of negation rose up in response.
' No,' they exclaimed, ' it is not worth living.
Everyone is miserable in the old mill-round of
routine and social bondage, in want of money
or in debt, weary of the falsehood and flimsiness
of all our words and works, of the groove we
cannot leave, of the phrases we are forced to
utter ; weary of striving and failing in the hope-

less quest of employment, where only favour
gains the prize, merit is set aside, and intellect
and worth have only the loss and the sorrow.'
So the vultures of discontent gnaw at the heart
of the age.   And there is but one supreme
remedy for these men of tired brains and
corroded lives and wasted energies, who pine
and perish in our overcrowded, overworked,
under-paid, exhausted social systems.   It is to
fling off the bondage of a worn-out civilisation
and start on a new career in a new country
with the audacity of youth and the certainty of
success.

Besides, if a large emigration is not organised,
and that London continues to increase by two
thousand a week (its present rate), we shall soon
have all England a monster factory, and all
London a model lodging-house laid out in flats,
rising like Babel to heaven, till both earth and
sky are obscured, and one will forget the green
of the grass or the form of a tree, and there will
be no divine solitude left any more for the artist
and for the soul-hunger of the painter and poet,
and the Ideal will die out, slain by the Real.

Mr Ruskin already complains that the rivers
of England run black with dye-stuff, and the
sky is heavy with smoke, and the scenery,
God-given and sublime, is sacrificed on all

sides to the devastating and destroying Moloch of trade.

It is a mistake, therefore—almost a crime—not to utilise the whole great English Empire for the ever-growing population with all its needs, spiritual and material. Every class and grade of society might be extensively weeded, so as to bring the numbers in London at least within a reasonable limit, in place of the five million that now encumber the soil of this mighty Babylon.

All younger sons waiting the abolition of primogeniture might go with advantage; all elder sons whose club bills are heavy and cigars unpaid; the hundreds of briefless barristers; all landlords whose incomes have been made over to their tenantry; all the waiters upon Providence in the courts of the publishers, the writers of magazine articles returned 'with thanks,' and all the brilliant young men who strive painfully after a shadowy income from the society journals by paragraphs and acrostics.

An emigrant ship freighted with this amount of fashion and genius would be an immense acquisition to the Australian world, as yet in the infancy of social scandal, gossip and thrilling romance; and the young aspirants for fame, in place of browsing on the thorns and thistles of Fleet Street and the Strand, will soon find grapes, and figs, and corn, and wine, and oil in abundance in the new land of their adoption.

Of course, with countless thousands a year, London is a delightful place; nothing equals it in the world for splendour and expense, for the magnificence of houses, horses and stately dinners.

But only about ten thousand persons in London can live this delightful life of love in idleness, with all its pleasant varieties and sins, and a million or so of toilers might be left to supply whatever they need; but the remaining three million might certainly be transplanted to a better field of action, with considerable advantage to themselves and society; where they could live and move and have their being as God meant them to be—useful and active members of the great human family.

For if one has no thousands a year, nor even hundreds, nor even so many pounds, and creditors become clamorous, and tenants get peculiar ideas about rent, and the young man of genius who has trusted to the chance of a prize for the best poem on the 'Christmas Robin' or the solution of the last acrostic finds the cheques from admiring editors few and far between, then the claims of civilisation seem rather vapid, the excitement lessens in intensity, and one almost begins to weary, if it were ever possible to weary of London enjoyment and society gossip.

At such times a morbid gloom covers life. and, with a blighted, hopeless, discouraged feel we painfully realise in our inner consciousness the melancholy fact that the dream of our youth was an illusion, and that we cannot suddenly spring to the summit of the social ladder and hurl down contempt and scorn on our rivals and enemies with superb disdain. Then is the moment for the emigrant commissioner to appear like a *Deus ex machinâ*. He offers land, and gold and work and triumph, and only asks in return the splendid daring of youth — for only the young should emigrate. Youth is for adventure, excitement, audacity and success ; and the glorious freedom of a new, magnificent country is a baptism of regeneration to the fevered victims of our vain, false social life, with all its 'venomous wind-sown herbage.' Amidst the strangeness and mystery of the untrodden wilderness, with its forests of cedar and sandal wood and mighty trees, within the hollow of whose trunk nearly a hundred men might find shelter, and the vast sheep-runs where a man may ride for two whole days and not come to the limit of his holding, the young generation of the wearied brains, the chilled ambitions, and wrecked hopes will find a new stimulus to exertion, a new excitement in existence, and certainly the chance of a better income than could be derived from even the most brilliant paragraph or the solution of the most involved puzzle in the acrostic column of the local journals.

They will miss at first, probably, the copious literature of the London press, and life will seem impossible without the solemn *Times*, the genial *Telegraph*, the soothing flatteries of the *Athenæum*, and the high-toned grace and courtesy of the society papers.

Yet even a rest from these things might be welcome and bring a tender calm and repose to the overtaxed brain. For that must be a land of pure delight where no demand is made on one for universal erudition; where it is not requisite to study all theories of government from Aristotle to Mr Gladstone while sipping the morning coffee; and where even the most exhaustless leaders would be worthless after a transit of forty days. In fact, one would be ashamed to be found reading them when the world had gone spinning on in quite another spiral of progress since they were written. Besides, the telegram, the literature of electri-

city, will adequately supply all knowledge summarised, and the whole history of the universe
can be cabled in a phrase. Even Mudie may
in future have his three volume novels wired
(without adjectives to save expense) in place of
packing them in tins as now for colonial consumption.

Literature is mainly the product of sorrow
and strife, and the Australians have had little
of either, so their intellectual efforts want, as yet,
force and pathos; they are deficient in despair
and aspiration, the qualities that create poets.
Nor have they any heroic traditions of a noble
and conquered race to be worked up into epics
and dramas. The Aborigines have no claim to
interest of any kind; they are evidently the
last decaying remnant of a low pre-Adamic
race, a mere slight advance of the kangaroo
towards the human, evidenced only by the
faculty of speech; they have no idea of God,
of religion, of government, or morality; no
words to express chastity, truth, purity or
shame. They are copper-coloured and hideous,
even brutalised-looking, like all inferior races.
They neither plant, nor sow, nor weave, nor
build; they live by fishing and hunting, and are
known to be cannibals. Their only garment is
an opossum skin torn from the animal, and

their only dwelling is formed of a skin hung to windward on the branches of a tree.

For six thousand years this race has had a trial on the earth, but has never made any advance in the scale of being. It is now, therefore, the manifest destiny of the great Adamic race to clear the world of these half-souled inferior types, as a forest is cleared of its poisonous undergrowth that the fair and goodly trees may expand and flourish, and take freely of the sustenance offered by earth and heaven.

To the English-speaking races above all have been given dominion and power over the earth, and what they have conquered they have a right to keep as their just and lawful heritage. And, if the suffering millions of the British Isles, the helpless, hopeless toilers in the exhausted plains and crowded cities of the Old World, have begun to find life all too bitter under the chill northern sky and the uncongenial constellation of the Great Bear, let them by all means arise in their might as the conquering sons of Japhet, claim boldly their portion of the broad earth, and go forth gladly and bravely to take possession of the fair and fertile land at the other extremity of the Empire that lies beneath the holy symbol of the Southern Cross.

THE VISION OF THE VATICAN.

(*A Study from Victor Hugo's Poem* ' Le Pape.')

'THE Lord of Tears,' 'the stormy voice of France,' as Tennyson finely designates the great Poet of Freedom, never denounced wrong and tyranny with more powerful invective than in this fine poem, which in its full expression of Sin and Sorrow, may be called 'The Drama of Humanity.'

Yet there is no actual life or movement, the scenes are visions only, supposed to pass before the mind of the Pope as he sleeps in his chamber in the Vatican, and they are flung as pictures on the mystic background of night and dreams, each vision representing a separate and distinct phase of human life.

First the kings of Earth pass before him in their purple splendour; then the Prelates in their sacerdotal pomp and pride, and after them the great stream of humanity sweeps by; the poor, the sinful, and the sorrowing ; the sheep without a shepherd hunted by the wolves; the tempted and the outcast; the victims of want and misery driven to crime by despair; and with fierce and scathing anathemas, the Pontiff in his dream denounces the sin robed in purple that receives the homage of the crowd, and contrasts it with the sin born of want and hunger that is expiated on the scaffold.

The language is bold and beautiful. Every line shows a terrible impatience of wrong, with an infinite disdain for the vain pomp of life; for the whited sepulchres filled with all uncleanness, and for all that is false, mean and shallow in our Social System. With superb audacity the poet rends the veil from the world's lies and the hypocrisy of the world's masters, and shows to King, Priest, and Ruler what they ought to be, but are not. The Priesthood had accused him of Atheism, he retorts by showing the pride and greed of the Church, and the darkness and bondage in which it holds men's souls; the Kings had accused him of stimulating Anarchy, he retorts by showing how every throne is set upon a writhing, tortured people, and every royal robe is trailed in blood.

But there is no reckless democratic rage in his teaching. No effort to reach regeneration through destruction.

After the denunciation comes the strong clarion call from the poet's lips arousing the people to a sense of the true uses of life, and the infinite beauty of those grand words—Light, Justice, Liberty—to which all heroic lives have been consecrated ; words that mean emancipation from ignorance, servility and oppression, and the uprising of a nation, or of a human soul into the nobler life of truth, dignity, knowledge and self-reverence.

Never is Victor Hugo's eloquence more powerful than when he preaches the great gospel of human brotherhood, the divine sympathy of man with man, which should be the moving principle of all social life; the true fraternity based on the recognition of the holy and eternal rights of man. 'Peace on Earth' is the Christ-word he would make a reality in its fullest sense, for in the new social state of which the poet dreams, there shall be no more war, nor oppression, nor crime born of want and misery; no pride of life while the people starve; no lights burning on the altar while the nations sit in darkness.

Help for the weak ; pity for the sinning ; justice for the wronged—these are the gifts he would have kings and priests lay on the altar of humanity, and above all, he demands Light

for the nations, even as light was first struck
from chaos before an organic world could be
evolved.

The first scene opens in the Pope's chamber
in the Vatican with a mystic invocation to
sleep : [1]—

> 'When weary men and women.   All who live
> And bear life's galling fetters on their limbs,
> Find peace and rest at last.

A voice is heard from Heaven :—

> Sleep now and take your rest
> From the dark tumult of a weary life,
> While like a silver lamp within a tomb,
> God's spirit comes to light the death-like form.

The Pope sleeps, and the Kings appear in his
dream and salute him.

> Hail to thee, Pope !   We are the Kings of Earth
> All powerful.   The Masters of the World.
> We stand upon the summit of all life,
> Supreme as Horeb or as Sinai.
> A mighty chain of mountains robed in light,
> Elect of God, and crowned by His own hand.

The POPE :—I see no summit in the world save one,
> And there God stands.   There is no king save God,
> But ye, what are ye?   Men like other men,
> Poor fleeting shadows of a passing day,

---

[1] There is no attempt at strict verbal accuracy in these
translations.   The object is simply to give an idea of the
tendency and scope of the poem by a free paraphrase of some of
the most striking passages.   The rich cadence of Victor Hugo's
verse none can emulate, ' The Thunder and the Music of the
Line,' but his strong thoughts are like golden sands, and may be
gathered without loss of lustre.   So I have endeavoured to
collect a few in this rough English casket, as they glittered by
me in the stream of his eloquence.

God's sacred sign is not upon your brow.
The mountains have the glory of the sun,
But ye are robed in darkness like the night.
Your thrones are vile.   Your purple reeks of blood.
There is for man but one throne, purity ;
One garment, love ; One law for all the world,
Light, Justice, Truth.   These are the Rights of Man.

The KINGS :—Yet thou, too, art a king, elected, crowned,
What is thy work on Earth?

The POPE :—To serve and love.
I blush to wear this triple crown of gold,
And dwell amidst my prostrate worshippers,
Like a dumb idol in this glorious shrine,
For what am I to be enthroned like God ;
Will not the Judgment come?

He advances to the portal of the Vatican and addresses the assembled crowd :—

Oh ! people trembling in these servile chains,
Help me to break your bonds of servitude.
See how I rend my royal golden robe,
And fling away these sandals from my feet,
Soiled by the lips of kings.   Now we are equal.
Now I go forth alone where Heaven may lead ;
Through storm or tempest, cloud, or sun, or rain,
To tread the stony places of the world,
And learn the mystery of suffering.
Romans, I leave you Rome !   Henceforth I reign
Over Christ's kingdom only ; deathless souls
Who bear the standard of humanity
Through want and woe and scorn and bitter tears.
Farewell to splendour !   People let me pass !
My path is in the track of Christ.   Farewell !

In the next scene the Pope, robed in serge, and, bearing a wooden crucifix in his hand, enters the eastern Synod.   The Patriarch in his golden robes and crown, surrounded by the bishops, rises from his throne to bless the people.

The PATRIARCH.—I bless the tribes and cities of the world ;
    The vales and hills ; the mountains and the sea ;
    All peoples ; earth and heaven.'

The POPE.—Rather bless hell !
    Ay, priest, bless want and misery and tears
    From broken hearts.   Bless tempted erring spirits
    Warring with wrong, yet falling in the combat.
    Bless the chained gangs of sullen tortured souls
    Made devils ere they knew their rights as men.
    Bless the faint hearts with only strength to suffer ;
    The wronged, the weak, the outcast and the sinning.
    Bless all for whom no lips have ever prayed,
    For these make up the sum of human life.
    Therefore, I say, bless hell !

The PATRIARCH.—Who is this man ?
    The Bishop of the West ?   Robed as for death !

The POPE.—And wherefore not ?   I mourn for human sin ;
    Still more for human pride and pomp like thine.
    Amid the world's great sorrows.
                         Cast aside
    This golden robe ; this glittering diadem;
    Thy velvet, damasks, pearl embroideries
    Are chords to strangle Christ.   These priceless gems
    Are tears of widowed mothers, orphan'd babes.
    Thy rubies are the blood-drops of the people.
    Doth not the pale Christ, with His crown of thorns,
    Rebuke thy sinful vanity and pride ?
    Look at the people crouching in their lair,
    Maddened by want and hunger.   Stalwart men
    Hunted by demons down the waste of years ;
    Wan, naked children sobbing in the streets ;
    Pale women bartering their youth for bread.
    Each hour a soul is passing to the judgment—
    Souls to be saved or damned !   Hast thou, O priest,
    Gone down to hell to save them ? taught the kings,

As priests should do, that sacred human rights
Mean honour, dignity and honest toil ;
The holy joys of home and innocence,
Not luxuries that make our toiling men
But devil's tools and ministers, because
The rich have vices and the poor want bread.
  Think you God's priesthood should look calmly on
While tyrants rivet chains, and evil laws
Degrade men to the level of a slave ?
You traffic in the sanctuary, and set
Your foot upon the people for a base,
That so the kings may trample them to dust.
Swing silver censers, let the incense rise
In perfumed clouds to heaven ! flash the blaze
Of all your altar lights upon the scene ;
You cannot hide the hideous wrongs of men
From God's swift searching glance.

The Patriarch and the Bishops vehemently express dissent.

The PATRIARCH.—Most saintly Pope,
  The laws are graven on brass, we cannot change
  The ancient form and usage of the Church ;
  Besides, the people like our splendid rites,
  The glory of the altar is their sun ;
  Our mitres flash like stars upon their eyes.

1st BISHOP.—And speak of kings with reverence ! their swords
  Cast the same shadow as the cross. God's temple
  Is founded upon kings ; if kings should fall
  God will fall with them.

2nd BISHOP.—Ay, in truth we know
  The people are but sheep and must be driven.
  Two powers only rule on earth—the priest,
  Head over all, and secondly the king.
  The ploughshare must be sharp to cut deep furrows.
  Leave it to us ! the priests of God know best
  How deep to cut that so good seed may grow.

3rd BISHOP.—And cease this cry of 'knowledge for the people ; '
  Books, schools and science ! What ! to make men think ?

They do not need to think ; dogma is everything.
Anathema on him who dares to doubt.
If they would reach us in the sanctuary
It must be on their knees.   Let us not fear
To burn up heresy as though a torch
Were flung into a field of straw.

The PATRIARCH.—Beware !
You drag the people down to an abyss
By this word Liberty.   It is perdition !
Bowed heads and humble hearts are all we need ;
Obedience to the priest and to the king.
To think, to judge, to reason, and to doubt
Is blasphemy, the primal sin of man,
That cost him Paradise ! and God will cause
All words and works to be accursed of those
Who preach this vain word Progress, to the people.

The POPE.—O Brother, clearer vision comes to me.
Can Dogma save them ?   From my splendid height
I looked down on a seething gulf of crime,
Black smoke of Hell that darkened all the land,
And poisoned even the incense on the altar.
Cries as of murdered souls went up to Heaven,
I saw the reign of Sin—the death of Innocence,
Vice set on high and Virtue in the mire ;
Christ's sheep left foldless and no shepherd near
To guide, to save, to comfort or to bless,
And make God visible to human eyes ;
So I have flung my earthly glories down,
What has God's priest to do with luxuries ?
Vain cheats foul frauds—I fling them to the poor !
I will not take my place amongst the Kings
Upon whose thrones rests everlasting darkness,
Kings, Princes, Pontiffs, Sovereigns, Cæsars ;
Weird shadows, hollow words, dead Phantoms robed
As living men, like idols in our churches,
False gods that brutalise the worshippers ;
Shall we take all the people's holy rights—
Light, knowledge, freedom, justice, happiness,
And sell them to the kings who build their thrones

On corpses, and fling hecatombs to death
To buy another jewel for their crown?
Trampling on Christ to honour Attila.

The BISHOPS.—Blasphemy! blasphemy!

The POPE.— Peace, proud prelates,
Peace! You outrage Heaven. O Christ, come down!
By all Thy seven wounds we plead to Thee.
Give back Humanity its rights, despoiled
Of all God's gifts and disinherited
By Kings and Priests. O people, women, children,
Have they not souls? have they not human rights?
Arise, O Priests, be on the side of God,
Build up a temple, holy, pure, sublime
With innocence and truth. The Lord Himself
Will be the light thereof, and every heart
A living stone on which God's name is graved.

The Patriarchs and the Bishops rise up tumul-
tuously and rush from the scene.

What! vanished like a vision of the night!
The phantoms fled that strove to be as gods!
So Babel fell through pride and vain ambition.
No priest—no temple! Must I work alone
In the dense darkness of this sea of sin?

A VOICE from Heaven—Have Faith and trust in God The
Lord is with thee!

The Pope leaves the Synod and goes forth on
his mission of charity and love; ministering to
all who sin and suffer, and bringing peace to
those who, through much sorrow, had began to
doubt on God. The people gather round him
with wonder while he speaks words of comfort
and compassion.

The POPE.—O People, I have left my royal stat
To learn the bitter sorrows of the poor

R

The woe, the wrongs, the agony, the tears,
The bitter desolation called your life.
Days without bread and nights made black with crime,
Unlit by any ray of love or sympathy.
Your wounds that none bind up, your souls none save ;
Your roofless homes, your fireless hearths, your cries
That stifle Hell, your sins that startle Heaven.
Come troubled hearts made mad by want and scorn,
I bring you love for hate.   I share your life,
And give you of my gifts—Light, Freedom, Hope ;
The knowledge of the birthright you have lost.
Come, soul-stained outcasts ; trampled, bleeding slaves,
Come all that men have shunned, that men despise,
That men have cursed.   Come all who weep and mourn,
I will present each suffering soul to God
And plead for ye before the Sacred Throne.

The crowd press round with tearful prayers.

A PASSER-BY.—What means this pauper multitude, Old Priest ?

The POPE.—I gather priceless treasure for the Lord.

In his dream the Pope beholds the building of
a Temple, while the Archbishop gives his orders
to the builders.

The ARCHBISHOP.—Bring jaspar, onyx, sapphire, porphyry ;
Make the gate splendid and the portal high,
That all may enter, all the people stand
Amid the glittering glory before God.
On the august facade flash forth in gems
The name ' JEHOVAH,' as if traced in fire.
Ring out the bells like choral harmonies
Sending vibrations to the inmost soul ;
And all things be in reverent order,
Christ's Bishop seated on his golden throne,
Christ in the stable ; and the holy Priests,
Let them have soft warm cushions as they kneel
To expiate your sins.

Bring costly gems,
Jewels for crowns, and flowers for festivals,
Gather all beauty of the earth and heaven,—
Statues like Gods, Madonnas, Prophets, Saints,
Divine as Raphael, strong as Michael Angelo!
Resplendent frescoes, all the walls ablaze
With the great story of Humanity;
The trees of Eden with their golden fruit,
And the fair Woman as she tempted Man,
The Builders piling rocks to mount to heaven;
Moses on Sinai, Christ on Golgotha;
Belshazzar's feast and Cana's wedding wine;
The wealth of kings, the splendours of the world
Were all too little for our holy Church,
Our altar and our priesthood.

The POPE.—   And the poor?
Will they find shelter in the winter night,
Amid your statues and your porphyries?

He mediates over the doom and curse that
rests for ever on human destiny.

Nothing but evil seems the law of life.
The People writhing in their dull despair,
And Princes, Nobles, Judges, Warriors, Priests,
All working out the tragedy of man.
The morning bids him weep, the night says die,
Sin, suffering, tears,—the sum of human life,
The doom of all the worlds, of all Creation.
This is the creed that all religions teach—
Sorrow on Earth, eternal fire hereafter!
Oh fatal shadow thrown on life from Hell
By rituals of falsehood and despair,
The dogma of Damnation!   Wrath and hate
Poured on our race throughout Eternity.
A darkened life, a dark abyss beyond;
If Man, a tortured, bound Prometheus;
If Angel, a thrice cursed Lucifer.
O helpless mortals in the grasp of fate,
Can we not claim some higher rights from God,
Then tears on Earth, and Hell for evermore.

A flock of shorn sheep pass by, while the wild
winter wind is raging.   The Pope regards them
with pity.

Poor shorn flock ! poor trembling shivering crowd!
What hand has shorn you of the sacred fleece
God gave you as your right, and left you bare
To the wild driving of the pitiless rain ?
Will not a curse rest on the impious heads
Of those who left you naked to the blast ?
So on for ever on through life's fierce storm
The mournful march of sad humanity,
Toiling and working, suffering, weeping, dying,
Naked while weaving royal robes for Kings,
Homeless while building granaries for others;
O People, ye who feed, clothe, nourish all,
The worthless and the idle are your masters,
They grind your lives down for their pleasuring,
Body and soul and brain, the rich seize all.
Where are the Shepherds whom the world calls Priests,
Can they not save you from the hands of those
Who take the wool and then will take the flesh,
O dark-winged angels of remorseless fate,
Why this eternal war upon the poor ;
Why must the shadow fall upon their lives
So darkly that it blots out all the sun?

The next scene is a battlefield, the Pope
stands between the two armies and speaks :—

What ! must we give these fields of living men,
To be mowed down, as wheat is by the scythe,
That Kings may make a footstool of the dead
To mount to thrones ?   They grasp at diadems,
And care not if the jewels drip with blood.
Aye, seize your lands, as wolves their living prey,
Send forth your fiat, bid the trumpets sound,
And tell the people 'tis a glorious thing
To die for Kings.   But I through blinding tears
I see your royal raiment trailed in blood,

The red plain strewn with dead and dying men,
The trampled fields, the burning villages,
The women weeping for their slaughtered sons.

He advances between the combatants with uplifted hand.

O People, break the chain, be strong and cease
To tremble at the shadow of a King !
Fling down your swords, and boldly say as men
' We will not sell our lives to purchase thrones,
And leave our children orphans for the sake
Of building up an empire for the Kings.'
And who are ye who do the murderous work,
And kill to order !   Men with brain and hand
And power and might, the workers of the world ;
True Titans of the Gods and of Humanity.
And yet you give your manhood to be ruled
By these poor phantom shadows called the Kings :
Who laugh and eat and hold high festival,
And gaily wreathe the cup of blood with laurel,
While earth is strewn with dead and drenched with tears.
You robe them, crown them, pay them from your toil,
Shrine them in gorgeous palaces, and then
Fall down before the gods of your own making.
Ye, the great movers of this vast machine
Called Human Progress !   Ye, who have upheld
By your strong work and arm the thrones of Kings !
Ye, root and leaves of the great tree of life,
Without whose aid the world would come to naught !
All-powerful People, mighty world-sustainers,
Rest but for one day idle, leave your work
And the whole fabric falls !
                              Beware, O Kings !
The People yet may know their power, and then
The cry of suffering humanity
For retribution of their ancient wrongs
Will startle earth, and reach the ear of God.
You stifle thought and bind revolt in chains,
And raise your scaffolds by your palaces
Amid the people's deep anathema ;

In every age the same environment
Of wrong, and wrath, and torture, and despair,
And edicts traced in blood.   But nothing done
To help the blinded, sinning, suffering soul,
To rise to human happiness through Love.
Each generation sends its bitter cry
Up to the silent heaven, ere it falls
Into the depths of everlasting darkness.
Yet still the wrong remains, the fetters gall;
The vengeance, and the sorrow, and the doom
Make human life more terrible than death.
The kings alone are sacred as the gods,
They set their feet on slaves, their thrones on tyranny,
And priests will preach to us of ' Right Divine.'
Tiberias before Christ !   Yet what are kings—
The Bourbon, Hapsburg, Brunswick, Romanoff—
But idols men create? and men can crush
If only they demand their rights as men.
But unjust laws, brute force, and grinding care
Stifle the life in nations : soul crushed slaves
They fall below the level of the beast,
While if they strive to give back blow for blow,
They're gagged and chained, and beaten with many stripes.

The Pope beholds a scaffold, and the executioner waiting for the victim.   He asks the reason.

The EXECUTIONER.—He slew a man.

The POPE.—And therefore you slay him.
A crime to expiate a crime !   Oh give
The sinning soul some time for penitence.
Repentance purifies, but not revenge.
What right have you, O Judges of the Land,
To take the life God gave, the sacred life
You never can restore, and call it justice ?
God is more merciful ; He sends old age,
The silent calm of passionless old age.
To bend the heart to penitence, and through
The sorrow for the sin work out salvation.
But you defraud the sinner of his rights,

And take from him the two sole ways of pardon—
Time and remorse.   God knoweth best the hour
To strike the doom of death.   Leave him to God.
Why should men dare to send a sinner hence
Before God calls him to the judgment seat,
With all the awful angels looking on;
Ere yet the baptism of grace had cleansed
The stain of sin that lies upon his soul?
If the dread past is shadowed dark with crime,
Give him the time to pray ; to lift his eyes
Out of the blackness of a ruined life
Up to the pitying heaven—where Christ stands
Pleading for sinners by the throne of God.
He may repent—give him the time for tears,
One hope, one gleam of pardon for the past,
One moment of God's sunshine on his soul,
Ere he is sent into the gulf of death.'

In the terrible misery of humanity the poet
finds the true cause that leads to crime ; and
the chief sin, he maintains, rests not on the
people, but on those who have driven the people
to despair.   Thus he justifies his fierce war
against the greed of kings, the pride of the
priesthood, and the selfish oppression of the rich ;
the purple and fine linen of Dives, while Lazarus
is dying at his gate.   In every age the great
world leaders have lifted the standard of battle
against wrong and tyranny, and Victor Hugo's
noble poem is a grand hymn of revolt against
the existing state of society with all its awful
contrasts and insolent luxury and bitter poverty
He sees,—

Down in the depths, a mass of living men
Groping and grovelling for their daily bread.

But Society with its vain traditions, and the
Church with its formal ritual, give no help to the
abject sorrow of the poor. Some great social
revolution seems necessary to lift them from the
moral and physical degradation of their darkened lives. Meanwhile the poet can but counsel
resignation :—

> Patience ! God's hour will come.   I lift mine eyes
> And see the Saviour standing by the throne ;

And he hears, though none heed,—

> Up from the depths, the ceaseless, bitter cry
> Of disinherited humanity.
> He will have pity, for He drained the cup
> Of human sorrow upon earth, and knows
> The soundless depths of human suffering,
> The bitte woes that tempt a soul to sin.

The last scene is entitled, 'The Entry to
Jerusalem,' in which is depicted the glorious
destiny of humanity as it might be, if Kings,
Priests and Rulers were true to their mission
as guides, teachers and saviours of the people.

> The Pope.—I preach to all men the great reign of Christ :
> Right, Justice, Truth ; the full equality
> Of man with man before the face of God,
> True liberty made perfect through the laws
> That guard the rights of others as our own.
> No ignorance, no fratricidal wars,
> No want, no misery, no darkened souls
> Made brutal by despair, therefore no crime,
> And if no crime no scaffold.
>   Let the rich
> Learn the true use of riches is to give ;
> And all who suffer by their own deep woe
> Teach pity for the sorrows of another.

The darkest fate can be made beautiful
By those great angels of Redemption, Grace,
Mercy and Love.   They raise the meanest life,
And give the darkest sunshine.
                      I have trod
The loftiest heights of splendour, King and Priest,
Yet now I give back Rome, and take Jerusalem,
The sacred, mystic city of the soul,
As my true heritage.   I leave the Vatican
And choose my place on Calvary with Christ,
To work and suffer for humanity.
The dying Christ, and not the living kings
Will give me power to raise the trampled crowd,
And make life's darkness luminous through love.
O workers of the world, true splendour rests
Not on the palace : 'tis a charnel-house
Where all divinest things lie slain and buried,
But in the holy strength of noble deeds,
The holy words—Truth, Duty, Sacrifice,
Fill Earth with light as Heaven is lit by stars,
And through the mournful mysteries of Fate,
Diffuse the Godlike grace of love and purity,
So shall true freedom come upon the earth.

The PEOPLE.—Father, we thank thee for Thy blessed words.

The POPE (awakening from his sleep).—What mystic visions I
    have had to-night !'

So ends this strange and powerful drama ; this divine dream of a noble soul filled with pity for the wrongs of man, but illumined by a sublime faith in the splendid possibilities of our race when redeemed and sanctified by Light, Justice and Freedom ; and that supreme moment of human history is reached when Humanity becomes at last the true Incarnation of Divinity.

IRISH LEADERS AND MARTYRS.

THE fervent nationality evoked by Moore's music and song at the opening of the century, and formulated afterwards into an immense political force by O'Connell, rose to a fever of enthusiasm in 1848, when a madness of lyrical passion seemed to sweep over the heart of the nation, and 'Young Ireland' sprang to manhood, splendid in force and intellect, earnest in aim, and stainless in life and act.

Amongst the new band of workers were powerful organisers like Gavan Duffy ; chivalrous leaders like Smith O'Brien ; orators like Dillon and Meagher ; and fervent apostles of freedom like John Mitchell, one of the boldest, bravest, and most noble-hearted of patriots. But the man, above all, whose words were a tocsin of Revolution, was the poet, orator and leader, Thomas Davis.

His whole public and literary career barely

exceeded four years, yet, in that brief time, he created a nation with noble, definite aims, and passionate resolves to achieve success.

A delirium of patriotic excitement raged through the land as these young orators and poets flashed the full light of their genius on the wrongs, the hopes, and the old heroic memories of their country; even the upper classes in Ireland awoke for the first time to the sense of the nobleness of a life devoted to national regeneration.

A *Gott Trunkenheit*, the ' Trunkenheit ohne Wein,' was on all hearts, the divine fanaticism of youth and genius. The leaders spoke as inspired men, and their words, like the words of the spirit, gave new life and power to every lofty purpose and high resolve. Even Trinity College struck the Irish harp to Hymns of Freedom, and the most popular poem of that era, ' Who fears to speak of Ninety-eight ? ' was written by a young collegian, afterwards a distinguished Fellow of the university ; and an eminent Irish Judge, but recently passed away, won his first laurels in literature by songs contributed to the national cause.

Another of the leading spirits of that day was Ferguson, afterwards Sir Samuel Ferguson, who illustrated all that was grand or tragic in the past by his splendid ballads ; and who flung the silken singing robes of the bard over the muse of Irish history; while Aubrey de Vere, the most cultured of all the Irish poets, crowned her with the golden diadem of his perfect verse.

The powerful ballads of Charles Gavan Duffy also achieved a rapid fame, and will for ever hold a distinguished place in Irish literature ; while as a song writer, John Francis Waller almost rivalled Moore in the melody and music of his words ; and his graceful and beautiful lyrics have the true mirth and pathos of Irish nature, blended and united. Denis Florence M'Carthy, the translator of ' Calderon,' wrote patriot verse that clashed like cymbals ; and Clarence Mangan brought treasures from every land and language to weave into the national minstrelsy ; while Carleton and Banim proved their claim to rank as poets, as well as the greatest amongst Irish novelists.

Nor was genius unrepresented in the other arts. Frederick Burton, the painter, now Sir Frederick Burton, first drank inspiration at the holy wells of Ireland, and has never known inspiration more fervent and glowing since he left their tree-shadowed mysteries for his English home ; and George Petrie's divine soul grew diviner amidst the holy ruins of the ancient

abbeys and the purple mist-crowned solitudes
of the Irish mountains; for love of country is
one of the great motive forces of the mind, and
the Irish have ever been singularly susceptible
to its influence as a stimulus to action.   Nor is
the influence evanescent, for the Irish people
have been tried through much suffering, yet
neither the prison, nor exile, nor broken hearts,
nor even death itself, could weaken the love
and reverence that binds them to their motherland.

In the great outpouring of the Spirit in '48,
not only the cultured classes, but the toilers and
artisans also, many of them were seized with
the poetic frenzy, and wrote and published
verses of singular merit and strong, rude power ;
for Celtic favour always finds its fullest expression in oratory and song.   The Irish, especially,
have a natural gift of copious and fluent speech.
They are orators at all times, but under the influence of strong excitement they become poets,
and in that stormy era, when every nation was
reading its Rights by the flames of burning
thrones, the Irish poets, mad with the magnificent illusions of youth, flashed their hymns of
hope and songs of defiance like a fiery cross
over land and lake, over river and mountains,
throughout Ireland, awakening souls to life that

might long have lain dead but for the magic incantation of their words.

Yet, the fate of many of those who made '48 a splendid moment in Irish history, was dark and tragic, and the flame lit up by patriot-passion died out in martyrdom.   The brave and brilliant Thomas Francis Meagher, the handsome and gifted young orator of the National party, was drowned in the waters of the Mississippi, and D'Arcy M'Ghee, the poet and statesman, met his death in Canada, mur-dered by some Irish fanatics who believed that he had given up nationality for place.   The high-souled Smith O'Brien, the descendant of kings, and venerated by the people as their chief, was tried and condemned to death, though the sentence was commuted afterwards to exile. He served out his time through the long weary years, disdaining to break his parole, and then returned to Ireland to die.   His last words were,—' My heart is broken.'

John Dillon, the impassioned orator, who could sway thousands to his will by the mag-netism of his presence, looking every inch the magnificent Spanish Hidalgo, with his dark eyes and raven hair, was doomed to prison and exile in the prime of his splendid manhood ; and came back only in long after years, a white-haired, mournful wreck, to rest in an Irish grave.

> He looked not like the ruins of his youth,
> But like the ruins of those ruins.

And John Mitchell, the all-powerful advocate of human freedom, suffered also the bitter martyrdom of exile, till youth, hope and energy were all crushed out of his life, and then he was permitted to return and see his native land once more. But the shadow of death was already on him, and he died just as the people, with all their old vivid love for the patriot-martyr unchanged, had elected him as one of their representatives in Parliament.

So they laid him in his Irish grave, with the shamrock on his breast, and never a truer heart, with its scorn of everything false, or a more powerful brain as thinker and writer, could be named amongst all those who have lived and worked and died for Ireland.

Clarence Mangan, one of the most remarkable of the gifted young race of that era, was found almost perishing of want in the streets of Dublin; and he died shortly after in the hospital whither they carried him.

Henry O'Neil, the artist and writer, to whom we are indebted for that truly splendid work 'The Sculptured Crosses of Ireland,' was sus-

tained chiefly by charity during the closing years
of his life, and his family, after his death, were
left almost in utter destitution.

But the list is endless of Irish genius left to
struggle hopelessly against the corroding cares
of life. A natural result when there is no kinship or sympathy between the rulers and the
ruled, no pride of race, no heroic memories, no
traditions of suffering common to both, yet the
the word *country* should be for ever sacred, and
lie at the base of all individual action and effort ;
for love of country is the divine force that can
alone war against the degrading tendencies of
mere material gain ; and no mental or moral
elevation can be attained by a people who do
not, above all, and before all, things, uphold and
reverence the holy rights of their Motherland.

THE POET AS TEACHER.

IT is one of Goethe's profound aphorisms, that
' Every day we should in some way renew our
impressions of the true and the beautiful by
a verse from some great poet, the sight of a
painting or a statue, or by a noble thought from
some heroic mind ; for the spiritual within is
ever in danger of being choked and suffocated
by the rank luxuriance of the weeds and thorns
that crowd our daily life.'   In this country,
however, Art has but few temples wherein lessons
of grace and beauty can be taught the people ;
nor can even the glorious book of Nature be
enjoyed by those who, with toiling hands and
ever lowered eyes, work day and night at the
loom of life to earn the scanty bread of sub-
sistence.

The poor in these rough northern climes have
little time for the dreamy musings over the
illuminated pages of Nature, to which the luxurious indolence of a southern existence gives

S

such full facility. The sunset and the cloud, the spiritual influence of dying day, or of night with her starry host; the grandeur of the lonely mountain, the song of waters, the choral music of the waving trees—all the beauty and melody of the world, is, in a great degree, mute and veiled to our weary toiling slaves of civilisation. But literature, in the full plenitude of its ennobling influence, can reach all classes, the lowest as the highest.

The words of man can permeate where the music of the forest trees never can be heard. In the cabin, the cellar, the factory, the mine, amongst the children of the cities or the plains, wherever there is a soul however darkened, the souls of other men can reach him; the divine thinkers of all ages may come in and sit down by him, though his dwelling be the meanest hut. The soul at least can 'build herself a lordly pleasure-house,' be the poor, toiling, material frame ever so lowly located. The duty of a government, then, is to ameliorate the condition of the people as far as possible by affording every facility whereby these angel ministers may pass to and fro amongst them. It is ignorance that degrades, not poverty or toil. 'That one man dies ignorant who has a capacity for knowledge, that I call a tragedy,' is

the deep and wise utterance of the great thinker
and philosopher—Carlyle. 'Every man,' he adds,
' even the meanest, is a priest sent to minister
in the Temple of Immensity.' And if the masses
of men everywhere have fallen from this high
birthright, so that the general characteristic of
the labouring classes has hitherto been that of
the lowest mental and physical degradation, the
cause and the consequences must be laid to the
charge of the ruling classes who for ages have
debarred them from the light and privileges of
knowledge. The truth seems only lately to
have dawned upon the English mind that education was necessary to build up a noble race of
citizens, and that every material advance, without a corresponding moral and intellectual progression, only ensured a vaster amount of crime
by increasing the facilities whereby all the tendencies of the lower sensuous nature could be
gratified.

Education forms the only counterpoise against
the low instincts of a darkened intellect. And
a world of gladness and blessedness dawns upon
the lowliest human life in proportion as the
clouds of ignorance are lifted. A noble thought,
then, brings joy, for the moral sense is elevated
to comprehend it. The beautiful can be unfolded everywhere from the sepal leaves of the

visible, and the awakened intellect finds endless
sources of joy in the study of the new-learned
harmonies between the laws of nature and of
spirit.

But the ignorance and darkness to which
Ireland was condemned, up to a very recent
period, would be scarcely credible, forming as it
does part of an empire whose wealth, power and
resources are inexhaustible, if it were not also
known that everywhere throughout her colonies
and her continents England has at all times
manifested the one uniform spirit—a love of
gain, and a neglect of souls.

Carleton, our great novelist, in the sketch of
his own youth prefixed to the last edition of his
Traits and Stories, thus speaks of the state of
education in his time :—

' In my youth I do not remember a single
school in a parish, the extent of which was ten
miles by eight. The instruction of the children
was a matter in which no one took any interest.
Education was wholly left to the hedge schoolmaster.'

And we have only to read Carleton's tale of the
' Hedge School ' for a melancholy proof of what
that education was, though the rich humour of
his description makes the sketch infinitely amusing. It is indeed coloured from the life, for at

this same Hedge School he himself, the 'Great Peasant,' received all the instruction of his early years. His trials afterwards in pursuit of knowledge were bitter, but one is half selfish enough not to regret them, since they resulted in that most pathetic tale of his *The Poor Scholar.*

Tracing, also, the abject misery and degradation of our people to this systematic neglect, even discouragement of education by all in authority, he says :—

' The Irishman was not only not educated, but actually punished for attempting to acquire knowledge in the first place, and in the second, punished also for the ignorance created by its absence. In other words, the penal laws rendered education criminal, and then caused the unhappy people to suffer for the crimes which proper knowledge would have prevented them from committing. It is beyond question, that from the time of the wars of Elizabeth, and the introduction of the Reformation, until very recently, there was no fixed system of education in the country. The people, possessed of strong political and religious prejudices, were left in a state of physical destitution and moral ignorance, calculated to produce ten times the amount of crime which was committed. Nor is it any wonder if poverty and ignorance combined

should give the country a character for turbul-
ence and outrage. The same causes would produce the same effects in any country.'

There is truly a deep analogy and intimate
connection between morals and education, holiness and intellect. The object of both is the
attainment of that ideal perfection which is God's
image stamped upon the soul, though obscured
for a time by ignorance and vice. Life has no
higher meaning than to evolve the inner subjective ideal in word, act and form—that is in
Literature, Morals and Art.

And to emancipate this higher nature should
be the noblest aim of all education. To
remove the mists of sense that stand between
the soul and the objects with which it has a
natural affinity. To reveal this soul itself in its
essential beauty and purity, as the statute becomes revealed slowly from within the block of
marble, according as the gross and exoteric is
disseeered from it. And as the lower nature is
annihilated, the soul will stand forth clearer and
and clearer, the human life reveal more and more
of the beauty, harmony, grace, and gentleness,
which is *love*, and the deep and intimate communion with the hidden and profound things of
the universe, which is *knowledge*. For all these
things are of the essence of the soul—they dwell

in it eternally—are not created, but revealed through culture and discipline. The thoughts of a great man do not startle us because they are new, but because they wake up what has long lain wordless in the deep infinite of our own souls.

This excellence, however, cannot become the law of a man's life until the lower nature is subdued, and made the slave not the master. This is the mystery of 'crucifying the flesh.' It is a deep truth which should be ever present to us, that each human being is a compound of two natures, the animal and the God—senses and soul, clay and ether ;. and the true task of life is to evolve the divine from the earthly.

Education, therefore, must contain a moral idea at the foundation, or it becomes only the ally of the senses. By the effect any work in art or literature produces on the mind, and by that only are we to judge its excellence—by the amount of emotion and the kind of emotion which it excites. Schiller's profound comment on St Peter's at Rome is, that its grandeur consists in making us grander. The proof likewise of the surpassing excellence of Handel's 'Hallelujah Chorus' is, that it excites the highest and sublimest emotion of the soul—worship. Our souls are elevated to his own level by a great

artist or poet, and we are for the instant equal
to Michael Angelo, Handel or Milton. When
the intellect and moral nature thus acts in con-
cert, striving together to realise the subjective
ideal, the result is the advancement of our entire
spiritual nature towards infinite perfection. It
is in a word *religion*, for this is the highest, completest term whereby we can express the eternal
asymptote or curve of the soul to God. But of
all forms in which the thought of man can be
incarnated, poetry is the one which produces
the most vivid and instantaneous excitement
upon the mind of youth. Children may be
insensible to the picturesque, to sculpture, music,
painting ; but no child-heart is proof against
a ballad. Impressions which last a life long are
often stamped upon the soul by the chantings
of a nurse. Thus Carleton's genius was first
awakened by the soft, sweet songs of his mother
to him in childhood in her own Irish tongue.
Poetry, therefore, must always form an important element in education, because it can be
made so powerful an auxiliary. It permeates
the blood, and tinges a nature for ever after.
Amongst the working classes especially, literature of feeling and imagination finds ready
access. No world of conventionalities rises up
as a wall between them and the spiritual, or

crushes them day by day with the dull, leaden weight of its petty forms. Their thoughts rush into space more easily than in higher, fettered, artificial modes of life. Their life-task and God —these are the two poles of their existence. How faithfully and trustfully they seem to realise him as a *Presence* in their daily life! referring all trials, fortunes and events to him alone—never thinking apparently of secondary causes—and this it is which often gives such dignity and pathos to the sorrows of the poor. Out of these elements, faith, simplicity, and an ever-present sense of the spiritual, is the true poetic spirit made, or the true recipient of poetry ; and so in the calender of genius one finds but few noble pedigrees. Here in our own Ireland have not Carleton, Banim, Griffin, Moore, all sprung from the people ? The star rests oftener over the manger than the palace. Knowing, then, the influence of poetry upon the people, and how readily they receive impressions through such a medium, one looks with interest on a collection of poems issued by the Irish Commissioners of Education, and intended expressly for the young hearts who are to be the working heads of the advancing age. The collection professes to range over a period of 500 years—from Chaucer to the present time—and

from such an ample field one might naturally
expect all that could elevate, inspire and in-
vigorate. Into this vast temple of thought,
where the words of the great of all ages are
collected—it is the office of the teacher to lead
the spirit - shrouded child, and guide him to
every shrine where the true divinity is worshipped ; to all that would excite the emotion
which produces noble deeds, all that would
appeal to the heart through the history, traditions, sorrows, hopes, aspirations of his native
land. After the knowledge of God, a wise
teacher would implant a Love of Country in
the heart of a child. It is the source of all the
noblest virtues, of those most difficult to attain,
for they rise on the ruins of narrow self-interest.
Thus would a noble, large-hearted race of men
be reared, fit to act when duty called them to
the great redemptive work of life, and a national
spirit fostered, which, re-acting against petty
party egoism, would make them one day worthy
of being intrusted with national power.

To unfold to the child all that is beautiful in
nature, and noble in life, is little, unless, at the
same time, you give him an object commensurate
with the great duties you teach him. The love
kindled for humanity must be concentrated where
it can act with power. The knowledge acquired

should find channels on every side to benefit
others, be a man's station ever so apparently
isolated and powerless, for to break down the
barrier-walls of self, and diffuse and expand the
riches of our own mind amongst thousands
around, raising them to the level we have
reached, no matter how gained, whether by
study or through sufferings, has in it something
glorious and godlike as an aim of life, and brings
to the soul something of divine felicity.

The true aim of all individual effort should be
national advance.　Our own land is the sphere
of our duties.　Here God placed us to dress it
and keep it; a vineyard of whose state he will
one day demand an account.　How a lofty self-
denying purpose can ennoble the lowest life,
poverty, rags and destitution, we know from the
history of many a holy saint :

> Sacrifice and self-devotion hallow earth and fill the skies,
> And the meanest life is sacred whence the highest may arise.

One of the many reasons, perhaps, of Ireland's
degradation is, that her gentry were never taught
to feel and act as Irishmen !　The fact of being
placed by God in this particular land, seemed
never to suggest the idea that they were to work
for it, or would have to render an account of
their stewardship.　Men and women are dead

and dying around us, whose hearts through life never throbbed at the word ' Country.' By some strange hallucination they strove by vulgar imitation to transform themselves into English, and then assumed they were identical, though England by many a bitter sarcasm showed how she scorned their pretended claim.

In the preface to the *Selections for Irish Children* these views of the paramount importance of inculcating a love of home and fatherland, are distinctly stated ; but throughout the whole collection we find no illustrations whatever of so just a theory. In connection with home or country there is not one verse which would strike into the young Irish heart ; and for the names even of our leading Irish writers we may search the volumes in vain. The general tone also is didactic and prosy, quite unfitted to attract the attention of youth. At that age fire and energy are demanded, as a translation into words of the first throbbings of the eager, buoyant, daring heart. Ethics must be taught in action, in a vivid picture language, in deeds of heroism that make heroes—of patriotism that kindles a glow which keeps burning a life long ; but patriotism is the word which, above all others, is excluded from the national education. Irish children, it seems, may be taught everything but

what regards Ireland. An instance of this is
given, by the compiler, in his introduction to the
Ballad Poetry.

For after going over all ballad history, from
Homer to Macaulay, through north and south,
east and west of Europe, and even crossing the
ocean to pay a tribute to the muse of the native
savages of America, he says that the national
poety of *Ireland* is a subject upon which he has
left himself *no space* to make any remarks.

Numerous instances have been already
brought before the public establishing the existence of this quarantine law against all things
Irish in the system of national education, yet
one would think that literature was too sacred
to be made the tool of politics. The thoughts
of genius are for all.ages, they are the inheritance, the rightful possession of a people. One
is ashamed to see them dovetailed to suit the
expediencies of a government.

Is it fair that native shrines should be veiled
before the eyes of the young child while he is
taught to kneel at those of other lands? Not
that sectarianism or one-sidedness in literature
should be mistaken for nationality. The mind,
like the mystic city of the Apocalypse, should
have portals open to all points of earth and
heaven, from which a thought, a holy and

ennobling thought may come. Heroism from all lands and of any age is still vital and will kindle heroism. We can sympathise with ' Horatius Cocles, who kept the bridge so well,' or with old King Pharamond, seated calmly by the burning pile to destroy himself if conquered ; but in this authorised collection for Irish children, of all the brave deeds our poets sang, of all the wild, beautiful legends of our land, which their verse made more beautiful, not a line is to be found. Holy memories and heroic traditions are the guardian spirits of a people. Why should national commissioners—

Scatter these angel guards, glorious and beautiful ?

There is an elevation by induction. Show a child what is worthy in his own race and he will strive to rise to it. Self-reverence is generated, for we reverence our own nature in that of our great men. Different literatures, truly, are but different languages in which one human spirit speaks. But each nation has a peculiar mental organisation. Each heart has its own idiom and ideas thus illustrated, a child will assimilate faster because they are congenial to his nature.

To rear a nation to its full stature upon foreign thought is impossible. Even in an

æsthetic point of view, nothing great or original
will ever result from it, much less will it awaken
the national pride, hereditary heroism or self-
respect, at all times necessary in those who
would advance their country's glory.   Germany
tried to live upon foreign thought for a hundred
years or more—English and French, or any
thought except their own—but nothing came of
it.   So at last, headed by those grand iconoclasts,
Lessing, Herder, Tieck, Goethe and others, they
threw down all the foreign idols, and went back
to drink at their own holy wells, their Sagas,
Mährchen, and wild lays of the Niebelungen.
There they found inspiration, and the free, native
tide of thought has ever since poured forth in
channels created by its own daring force—the
only fitting channels for that wondrous German
mind, at once the profoundest and most imagin-
ative of Europe ; while, on the other hand,
by stifling the free utterance of native thought,
the literature of modern Italy became the
most meagre and artificial of Europe—for the
Austrian forbade the words country, independence or freedom to be uttered by the subject
people.   There is a magic might in song.   All
rulers and despots know this well.   Napoleon
found its power, when the chorus,—

Sit sollen ihn nicht haben, derfreie Deutsche Rhien !

made all Germany fly to arms for the War of
Liberation. The songs of the poets become
swords in the hands of the patriots. Can it be
in fear of this transmutation, that Irish song
is not flung into the furnace of young hearts?
One can only hazard an hypothesis for the
cause of this singular omission ; but the *fact*
can be easily proved by merely looking over
the index of the selections. In the long list
of poems on home and country, there is but
one by an Irishman, and that merely displaying
individual, not national feeling—it is, ' Our
Native Valley,' by Griffin—although the compiler states in the Introduction, and justly, that,
' On the love of home is founded that of country,
and unless this first of affections is inculcated
the heart must ever remain selfish, desolate
and cold to all social and patriotic feelings.'
His illustration of these admirable sentiments
is by teaching the poor Irish child to chant
' The Stately Homes of England.' France might
as well make ' Rule Britannia' her national
song, in place of the ' Marseillaise,' or America
rear her youthful population upon ' The British
Grenadiers.'

In the list of ' Songs and Lyrics ' there is but
one by Moore, the chief of our poets and our
national glory and that the least characteristic

of his melodies. However, in compensation, we
have ' Ye Mariners of England ' and ' Scots wha
hae wi' Wallace bled,' which, though excellent
poetry, could scarcely vibrate through an Irish
heart like Moore's grand and solemn appeal,—

> Let Erin remember the days of old,
> Ere her faithless sons betrayed her.

In the list of the ' Social and domestic affections,' not one Irish name is to be met with.
Not a line from Banim's iron verses, strong
and sinewy as a peasant's arm, and passionate
as his heart. Nor from Griffin's mournful muse,
filled with that deep tenderness yet plaintive
orientalism of resignation so characteristic of
Irish sorrow. How in that poem of his, ' The
Mother's Lament,' one sees the poor old for-
saken, desolate, bereaved-one rocking herself to
and fro, by the chill hearth of her ruined home,
while she chants—

> My darling, my darling, while silence is on the moor,
> And lone in the sunshine I sit by our cabin door ;
> When evening falls quiet and calm over land and sea,
> My darling, my darling, I think of past times and thee !
>
> My darling, my darling, God gave to my feeble age,
> A prop for my faint heart, a stay in my pilgrimage ;
> My darling, my darling, God takes back his gift again,
> And my heart may be broken, but ne'er shall my will complain.

Do not these genuine outpourings of an Irish

T

heart call a rush of tender tears to the eyes, which the cold, cultured extracts from ' Gertrude of Wyoming,' given in the selections, never could awaken?

Amongst the ballads also, a species of composition in which Ireland has won a world-wide fame, there are but two representatives from our country—Moore's ' Lake of the Dismal Swamp,' and ' The Faery Thorn' by Ferguson. The omission of all other distinguished Irish names cannot, however, arise from ignorance; for in his simple way of always making his prose bear testimony against his verse, the compiler assures us of the deserved popularity of Banim, Callanan, Lover, Davis, etc., amongst the modern Irish writers in this particular department, yet no extract appears from any one of them; and throughout the whole work, not a single line from Davis is to be found. The grand and glittering ballad of ' Fontenoy,' every verse flashing like swords in the sunshine, would give the heart of youth a healthier action, one would think, than ' Sweet William's Ghost.' Or that other by Davis, where the verse bounds on fierce and beautiful as a panther,—

> Oh! for a steed, a rushing steed, and a blazing scimitar,
> To hunt from beauteous Italy the Austrian's red hussar,

> To mock their boasts,
> And strew their hosts,
> And scatter their flags afar.

Oh! for a steed, a rushing steed, and dear Poland gathered round,
To smite her circle of savage foes, and hurl them to the ground ;
> Nor hold my hand
> While on the land
> A foreigner foe was found.

Or is 'The Child and Hind,' another of the selections, better teaching for the men of the future who are to war and work against the darkness and bigotry of ages than the spirited nationality and noble moral of 'The Irish Chiefs,' which thrills like a *sursum corda* through the frame.

Oh! to have lived dear Owen's life, to live for a solemn end,
To strive for the ruling strength and skill God's saints to the chosen send ;
And to come at length with that holy strength the bondage of fraud to rend,
And pour the light of God's freedom in where tyrants or slaves are denned.

Or 'The Muster of the North,' by Gavan Duffy, with its fast and fiery rhythm, like the rushing of horses over a rocky causeway ; or that spirited Orange chant of 'The Maiden City,' by Charlotte Elizabeth, coloured with the memories of the other Ulster race, beginning,—

> Where Foyle his swelling waters
> Rolls northward to the main,
> Here, queen of Erin's daughters,
> Fair Derry, fixed her reign.

> A holy temple crowned her,
>   And commerce graced her street,
> A rampart wall was round her,
>   The river at her feet;
> And here she sat alone, boys,
>   And looking from the hill,
> Vow'd the maiden on her throne, boys,
>   Would be a maiden still.

Ballads like these light up courage and hero-ism. A great heart speaks in them, and the child, for the moment, is transformed into the hero. But, alas, native heroism is a *taboo'd* sub-ject to the young national scholar. He may sing of Wallace wight, and the triumph over the Armada, but must not dare to tell how at Fontenoy—

> Right up against the English lines the Irish exiles ran—

and conquered too. But leaving these exciting ballads aside, why is there no illustration of Carleton's thrilling genius given? Would not the exquisite faery music of his legendary ballad of ' Sir Turlough '—

> The bride she bound her golden hair—
>   Kileevy, O Kileevy !
> And her step was light as the breezy air,
> When it bends the morning flowers so fair,
>   By the bonnie green woods of Kileevy ! —

have been a bitter poetical model, and more fitted for a place in an authorised collection for national purposes, than the infantile lispings of

the Misses Davidson, of America—'The Shout-
ing Cuckoo,' or the feeble, flimsy fripperies of
the 'Keepsake Era'?

Then we have numerous specimens from a
poet of Blackwood, called 'Delta'; but of the
learned, original mind of Clarence Mangan,
there is no trace whatever. Poor Mangan;
who spent a weary, sad life illustrating all
literatures from Ireland to Irân! and who lives
consecrated in the martyrology of genius, though
allowed no place in the Pantheon of Marlborough
Street, amongst the Peabodys and Patersons,
and Polehills and Wasthills, and Wiffens, and
Wilcoxes, and other poets of such-like strange
and uncouth appellations whom the compiler
delights to honour, though where he discovered
them (particularly Wiffen, author of 'The Shout-
ing Cuckoo') is the grand mystery of the book.
It is so sad in all the wide world not to know
where to look for Wiffen!

But the selections even from the best poets,
are as unfortunate as the omissions. Moore, for
instance, seems more like an improved version
of Isaac Watts than the impassioned bard of
Ireland—the quotations from him being principally of sacred pieces, and one 'To a Grass-
hopper.' From Keats, 'flushed all over with
the rich light of poetry,' but one poor extract on

'Autumn.' Were there not 'Madeline' and the 'Pot of Basil,' and these two exquisite odes to a 'Grecian Urn' and a 'Nightingale' to choose from? But of these not a word.

Then not a line from Motherwell, but an interminable number from that dull Montgomery, beginning with 'Autumn,' too. All he ever wrote is not worth Motherwell's 'Jeannie Morrison.' No rich and gorgeous harmonies of Tennyson's from 'Locksley Hall' or the 'Lady Godiva.' No gleam of that sweet vision the 'Queen of the May.' Or, 'Mariana in the Moated Grange.' Only two extracts upon 'Autumn' likewise.

'To a Bee,' 'To a Primrose,' 'To Autumn,' ditto, ditto, ditto, is the staple commodity appended to every name great and small down the index.

We turn to Wordsworth,—but find only Daisies and Daffodils. Not one tinge of sanctuary splendour. No 'Intimations of Immortality,' not a 'Palm Leaf' from Monckton Milnes. Yet, how beautiful is his poem, 'The Flight of Youth.'

> Alas ! we knew not how he went,
> We knew not he was going—
> For had our tears once found a vent
> We had stayed him with their flowing.

It was as an earthquake when
We awoke and found him gone,
We were miserable men,
We were hopeless, everyone !
His impassioned eye had got
Fire which the sun has not—
Silk to feel and gold to see
Fell his tresses full and free,
And engarlanded with bay
Must our youth have gone away.
Though we half remember now,
He had borne some little while
Something mournful in his smile—
Something serious on his brow;
Gentle heart, perhaps he knew
The cruel deed he had to do.

And that other sweet poem of his entitled
'Moments'—

I lie in a heavy trance,
With a world of dreams without me,
Shapes of shadows dance
In wavering bands about me;
But, at times, some mystic things
Appear in this phantom lair
That at most seem to me visitings
Of truth known elsewhere.
The world is rich, these things are small,
They may be nothing, but they are all.
A sense of an earnest will
To help the lowly living,
And a terrible heart thrill,
If you have no power of giving
An arm of aid to the weak,
A friendly hand to the friendless,
Kind words, so short to speak,
But whose echo is endless.'

These are verses to set as jewels in the heart ;

but while the noblest poets are ostracised, we find plenty of Mickles and Millars and Mudies, and what they said.

Hogg's name is there, but no bright fragment from his ' Bonnie Kilmeny,' the sweetest poem of modern Scotland. From Coleridge—the visionary Coleridge—we have only ' Lines to a Young Ass,' not a line from ' Christabel,' or ' The Ancient Mariner,' the poem above all others to excite the heart of youth. And Elizabeth Barrett Browning, the great poetess of England—of the world — is not even named. Yet that noble poem of hers, ' The Cry of the Children,' so full of beauty and agony, of tenderness and sublimity, is excluded to give room for Miss Eliza Cooke's lines to a Buttercup, and Miss Hannah Golds' to a Crocus.

There are pale young faces enough around us, marred with want, misery and famine, and sad young hearts from desolated homes, to realise Mrs Browning's mournful description :—

> Do you hear the children weeping, O, my brothers,
>   Ere the sorrow comes with years ?
> They are leaning their young heads against their mothers,
>   And *that* cannot stop their tears.
> The young lambs are bleating in the meadows,
>   The young birds are chirping in the nest ;
> The young fawns are playing with the shadows,
>   The young flowers are blowing toward the west ;
> But the young, young children, O, my brothers,
>   They are weeping bitterly !

They are weeping in the playtime of the others,
  In the country of the free.

And well may the children weep before you ;
  They are weary ere they run ;
They have never seen the sunshine or the glory,
  Which is brighter than the sun.
They know the griefs of men, but not the wisdom ;
  They sink in the despair without the calm,
Are slaves without the liberty in Christdom,
  Are martyrs by the Pang without the Palm ;
Are worn as if by age, yet unretrievingly,
  No dear remembrance keep ;
Are orphans of the earthly love and heavenly —
  Let them weep ! Let them weep !

Poor L. E. L. is somewhat better treated. But she has written verses more attractive to youth than some we find here ; for instance, her spirited, clanging lines on the death of Alexander, surrounded by

His silver-shielded warriors
The warriors of the world !

And ' The Graves of a Household,' by Mrs Hemans, might surely have claimed a place, of which Monckton Milnes says so beautifully—

There's not a line but hath been wept upon.

Of Shelley's ' Sensitive Plant ' there are only half-a-dozen verses given. Its fine sensibilities no doubt shrank from keeping company with a Mr Hurdis, who says,—

I love to see the little goldfinch pluck
The groundsell's feeble seed, and twit and twit and twit.

Neither is the arrangement the best that could have been chosen for the advantage of students. The classification by subjects is fatiguing in the extreme. One grows wearied by the monotony of a series to similar objects, or on the same subject. Dr Johnson speaks all our feelings when he says,—'One ode, sir, is well enough, but half-a-dozen of them together makes one very sick.' Beside the poems ranged under different metaphysical heads, we have an animal series (so long that it seems a rhymed bill of lading from the ark) and a vegetable series, and another to fish. Surely, none but graziers from a cattle show could get through poems to a ram, to a lamb, and to an ass, following in consecutive order as they do here. Then come a great number to cuckoos, but these all appear to be by Wiffen; and amongst the ichthyological specimens we find a sonnet to a gudgeon, by some anonymous writer, the compiler actually leaving out the names of such men as Davis, Carleton and Mangan, to make room for a sonnet to a gudgeon!

In addition to the weariness which such an arrangement induces, it deprives the student of the opportunity which a chronological order gives for becoming familiar with the eras of the language, and the mental history of the

nation at each successive period. The Saxon,
the Latin, the French, and the Teutonic styles
of composition in English Literature are as
clearly defined as the successive orders of
architecture ; but these distinctions of style,
and the psychological phenomena of which
they are the exponent, are wholly lost by the
want of a chronological arrangement. The
poetry of an age is generally the completest
expression of the mind of that age, the ultimate
and most perfect formula to express the height
to which thought has reached. It incarnates
the highest ideal to which the soul of humanity,
viewed in its unity, had sprung, and gives
definite form to those vague perceptions of the
new regions of thought to which it is travelling.
It is not merely the result of the spirit of an
age, but the spirit itself. Not alone the actual,
but the tendencies. Poetry is, in fact, the
chanted spiritualism of an age ; whether that
spiritualism be as full of faith and earnestness
as the 16th, and first half of the 17th century ;
as frivolous, false and materialised as the 18th ;
or as daring and transcendental as the philosophic creeds of our own day. Whatever faith
or hope exists in any age, will be found con-
densed or sublimated in the poetry of that
era. But from the arrangement of these selec-

tions no definite idea can be gained of the peculiar characteristics of each successive century.

The biographies of the poets form the third volume of the work. They are interesting, useful and well executed, and it must be acknowledged that wherever the editor speaks in his own person, it is with sense and judgment. Indeed, his prose displays so much of the qualities in which his selections are deficient, that we must impute the failure of the latter to some stern political necessity; some dark and secret threatenings, some official baton suspended over his head, which forced him, in defiance of all good taste, to send forth a collection which almost justifies Hallam's sarcasm on these works in general, that they seem compiled on the principle of excluding everything which is good.

THE TWO ARTISTS.

A SKETCH.

(*From the Spanish.*)

THE STUDIO.

IN one of the narrowest and most obscure streets of Seville, there stood, in the year of grace 1616, an old-fashioned house, which, in consequence of repeated addition, subtraction and multiplication of architecture, could in no way have been recognised by the ancient builder, who, years before, probably with much joy, had eliminated his fundamental idea of beauty in its creation.

The house consisted of two storeys, if the upper half may be dignified by such a title, being nothing more than a species of loft with an earthen floor, and low raftered roof, to which you ascended by a ladder. But this loft, or garret, or den, is precisely the only part of the house in which we are interested. However, to gratify laudable curiosity, we state that the remainder of the *Domus* consisted of a parlour, a small kitchen, a large paved court, and a villainous stable for one horse, uniformly empty; and we state the fact now respecting the stable, that the subject need not again be resumed.

The den (we prefer the briefest appellation) had two windows—one looking on the street, and the other on the paved court at the back. When you raised your head perpendicularly, after ascending the ladder, and projected it through the trap-door which served for entrance, you beheld various pieces of canvas, pictures and prints, some hanging from the wall, others strewed on the floor, evidencing at the first glance, that the idea of symmetry in the arrangement could never have entered their owner's head. Some were resting on the side, others suspended from a corner, or dangling negligently, according as the nail from which they hung was placed at a greater or less distance from the centre of gravity ; while unfinished pictures, bold sketches of vivid power and imagination, and studies of the human form in every stage of transition, were blended on floor and tables with equal disregard of harmonic arrangement.

A small bookshelf was suspended from the wall, containing some ten or twenty volumes of poetry and scholastic philosophy, along with Albert Durer's *Symmetry of the Human*

Frame ; Bexalio's *Anatomy ;* Daniel Barbara on *Perspective ; Euclid's Elements ;* and other mathematical and artistical writers. Then there were piles of rough crayon outlines, caprices of a painter's brain ; half-sketched landscapes, daubed and spoiled, as was evident from the contemptuous manner in which they were thrown into a corner ; and beyond, a large oak chair, on which lay papers, drawings, etchings, a hat with a rather attenuated feather, a faded doublet, and a jerkin of silk, one sleeve of which hung over the chair, reposing calmly in a small tub of water which *par hasard* lay near. A pestle and mortar, for grinding colours, stood on the table ; and towards the centre of the apartment, near one of the windows, was placed a large easel, over which a canvas was extended, on which fell a good light from the north, entering in at the left side. The window was judiciously shaded, admitting only one bright, full, direct ray from the top, which fell upon the glowing olive face of a peasant boy, who, seated in a grotesque attitude, displayed two rows of the whitest teeth in all Seville, sharpened, no doubt, by the bread of Toledo, in an affected laugh of such broad extravagance, that the most afflicted spectator would have been moved to hilarity. But, by a singular con-

tradiction, the only spectator present did not in the
least participate in the mirth. He was a young
man, of some eighteeen or twenty years, with a
grave, earnest expression, pale bronze complexion, and large deep eyes of enthusiasm and
genius. He stood before the easel, a palette in
one hand, and brush in the other, copying, as it
seemed, that reckless, extravagant laugh of the
sunny-cheeked peasant-boy; but there was no
inspiration in the work, to judge from the con-
tracted brows, compressed lips, and quick, convulsive movement of the artist. Twice or thrice
he drew back to contemplate his progress—his
eyes wandering rapidly from the model to the
copy. Then he touched, and retouched, and
obliterated and renewed; but the result of all
the manipulations was only a violent exclama-
tion—' I swear to—,' and here he stopped like a
good Christian, to consider whom he should
swear to. ' Valame Dios,' he continued, ' who
can imitate such tints?' and, after some apparently violent efforts to control his rage, he
seized the brush, and drawing it from top to
bottom right through all the moist colours,
succeeded in producing—a beautiful rainbow
certainly—but by no means anything approaching to the original design of the picture. Not
content with this, he aimed a violent blow at the

very centre of the canvas, causing a large triangular rent, and exclaiming, without the least scruple of reserve this time—'Voto à Dios! no mortal man could give those tints,' he flung away palette and brush, and threw himself into the large oak chair, over papers, doublet, jerkin, hat, and all, in the most utter contempt of their claims on space. Then, covering his face with both hands he remained motionless, in a pale trance of suffering, agony and despair, as if he were dead—the suffering, the despair of Genius who sees Heaven, but cannot ascend to it.

The glowing boy, who had served as model, without saying a word, or appearing at all astonished at his master's frenzy, closed his lips over the two strong white rows of teeth, and, seating himself on the ground, drew a huge piece of black bread from his bosom and commenced eating it with a voracity that proved how much he had been longing to cultivate its acquaintance. Occasionally he took a furtive look at the master; but, observing no sign of motion, when he had finished the bread and smacked his lips lusciously over the last morsel, he slid from the studio, and the artist was left alone.

Tranced in thought and misery, silent and still sat that despairing painter, giving no sign

U

of life, save a convulsive twisting of the hands.
Once he raised his head and looked wildly
around him, then pressed both hands upon his
brow, as if to repress some horrible thought.
Thus passed the day, and he ate not; thus
passed the night, and he slept not.   When
morning dawned however, he rose, with sadness
indeed, still upon his countenance, but not
despair—took his hat, with the crushed, broken
plume, wrapped his large mantle around him,
curled his nascent moustache with a natural
and unconscious movement of vanity, though
his dry and hollow eyes betrayed the sleepless
night, and then, crossing himself devoutly,
descended the ladder to the street.

THE INSPIRER.

He was a good Christian; a Christian of the
sixteenth century, though the seventeenth had
begun, and therefore his steps were first bent
towards the neighbouring church.   There he
heard mass, and was preparing to quit the porch,
somewhat tranquillised, when a hand touched
him lightly, and a well-known voice saluted him
with a 'Good-day, Señor Diego.'

The person who addressed him was a tall,
fine-made old man, of about seventy, with dark
complexion, marked, bold features, that once

must have been eminently handsome; large vivid eyes—eyes of genius, that flashed with daring and poetry, revealing all the ardour of a soldier and enthusiasm of an artist. The mouth was small and sunk in from loss of teeth, but age was no way discernible in the noble and easy movement of the dignified speaker.

Truly his mantle was worn threadbare, and the doublet, though slashed and broidered, was in no better condition than his friend's; but though you could see poverty in the twanging of a bow-string, yet his half-military costume was worn with a certain air of self-respect, and the soldier was still discernible by the handsome sword at his side, and the very mode of wearing his plumed hat.

It was a strange sight the meeting of those two men; one entering life, the other leaving it; one all hope, the other all memory; but both fierce combatants with destiny; both looking out on a cold world with eyes through which glittered a burning soul, a genius of fire, and a volcanic imagination. You could read there a life that enthusiasm was wasting as if with an iron file, and this through the prism of the future in the youth, through the veil of the past in the old man. He who looked on them but once, would have distinguished them from the vulgar herd, and exclaimed, ' a mystic past and future lies hidden beneath those fleshy masks— a heaven or a hell.'   For the youth, suicide or glory ; for the other—but the other had already fought a hundred combats with life and destiny —ay, and had conquered.

And, in truth, that old man was a poet, a grand poet ; though poor and neglected, save by some finer spirits, filled with genius and enthusiasm, who worshipped the wondrous intellect within him.   Our young painter knew him well, and loved and respected him as a profound philosopher and a brave soldier.   His verses were engraven on his heart, and many a trova of them had he recited to the young students of Seville, who shouted back their wild applause.

'Why this pallid cheek, Diego ? ' exclaimed the old man, ' those heavy eyes.   Why consume thy life, which is a prophecy of glory; thy heart— tell me, boy, what means this ? '

' It means,' said the painter, interrupting him quickly, ' a night of vigil, of weeping, of torture, of despair, of madness,' and he grasped the arm of his companion, and groaned heavily.

' What ? first love, is it ? ' said the old man with interest.   ' But, no, there is a wilder light burning in those eyes.   Tell me, young man, what has happened ? '

' What has happened ? Lost my hopes of glory
—burned my wings—fallen—fallen to earth.'

' Ha! thou hast undertaken something beyond thy powers. Thou shouldst wait for the
moment of inspiration, child.'

' No, no ; there is a line, a boundary I can
never pass, and yet, to be confounded with the
rest !—'

' Peace, boy. *Thou* wert not born to be confounded with the crowd. No ; raise thy head
—raise it thinking of glory.'

' Yes, I dreamed of glory, and to you I owe
those dreams which have destroyed me. I must
have fame or die. No base, corroding death-in-
life for me ; and now—who will give me back
the wings to mount ? '

' Have faith in thy own powers,' said the old
man, with the fire of enthusiasm, as he placed
his hand on the young painter's shoulder and
looked into his eyes, burning with genius and
poetry, ' Have faith ; thou knowest not the
hidden treasures of thy soul. Strive. *I* promise thee immortality.'

' It is in vain ! ' replied the youth, with apparent indifference. ' Glory has lost her illusions. I should perish but embracing a cloud,'
and he remained silent ; then added,—' But you
Senhor—you, too, have dreamed of glory ! You

have worshipped her in every form, and what—
what has been the result ?   Is this threadbare
mantle glory ?   This faded doublet ? '

' True,' said the old man, with sadness, ' true,
I am weak, poor, persecuted ; behold my glory ;
all that I have obtained from the idol I caressed,
adulated, deified !   Thou hast rebuked me, O
God ! '   And he bent his head, but after a moment raised it again, with the haughty fire of a
soldier and a poet.   ' Yes, I am poor,' he exclaimed, ' poor but honoured, and the visions of
my genius—the beings I have created, like a god,
with their virtues, vices, passions, follies at my will
—these phantoms into which I have breathed the
breath of life—this world which has sprung up at
my feet, with all its fantastic colouring, its illusions, its deliriums, its delights ; in which I wan-
der free as air and, god-like, create and destroy
with a word, a thought—tell me, who can deprive
me of this world ?   Does it not compensate for
all the agonies of life ?   What glory equals that of
a man who wanders amidst his own creations ?
Tell me, does it not equal the glory of a god ? '
And the deep lines on his high brow seemed to
pass away, and his eyes streamed with the
double light of genius and of youth ; and with
his noble head thrown back, his proud glance of
conscious power, that seemed to measure earth

with the sceptre of heaven, he looked no longer
a man, but a spirit, a god—yet more, that which
comprehends them all—a poet! The true poet,
as he stands transfigured by the light of inspiration.

The young painter felt himself dominated by
that eagle eye, those eloquent lips, and bent his
head to the ground, ashamed of his own weak
petulance, in silence and humility.

'Come,' said the old man, 'let us return to
thy house—courage for the soul and work for
the hand, and never name despair again—
come!' And the youth followed him as docile
as a lamb.

THE PORTRAIT AND THE PROPHECY.

The studio was in the same state as we left
it when these two men entered, looking like
father and son.

'Where is the canvas?' said the old man.

'Here,' replied the youth, lifting up the torn
disfigured object of his rage and despair from
the earthen floor.

'What! not content with this? Thou hast
destroyed a prodigy. What life! what vigour!
The face laughs, the whole figure laughs. What
colouring, what boldness of outline. Ah! this

medium tint is the only blemish, touched and
retouched till thou has spoiled it, boy.'

'Ah!' replied the painter, 'it is this which
ruined me, which caused my despair.   I saw
the tint wandering round the lips of the model,
uniting but not blending with the shadow, and
and I had the idea in my head but could not
execute it.   Have I not cause for despair?'
he added, weeping.

'No, no, young man; leave the vulgar track;
cease to imitate; follow thy own inspiration.'

'Inspiration!   What can I invent?   What
colouring that Titian has not already produced
with so much softness and harmony? Alas!
Corregio, too, with his enchanting grace, his
exquisite taste, the roundness and finish of
his forms, and his virgins—! My imagination
that you talk of, what serves it? Has not
Raphael's exhausted everything that is divine
in expression and beautiful in idea? Oh, why
was I born so late? What is there left to me
in the world of Art?'

'To imitate Nature.   All others have idealised
her—some to embellish, others to degrade.   Do
thou paint her as she is, with her divine beauty,
her venerable majesty, conferred on her by the
Most High, with all her capricious defects, her
strong, decided tints, without omission, without

addition; and thy inspiration, thy pencil, will do the rest. Then, then, hope for glory, but not for happiness. No, no; dream not of that. Dost thou tremble? Dost thou fear envy, persecution, the scorn of ignorance, the malice of rivals, the neglect of the world—dost thou hesitate to sacrifice happiness upon the altar of glory — thou art no artist. Break thy pencil.'

'No, no,' exclaimed the youth, with enthusiasm, and his spirit agitated, as by a tempest, with the words of the old man. ' Give me but fame, give me immortality, and I accept every evil life can offer. I defy them,' and he raised his head proudly, and it seemed as if Hope, evoked by the talismanic words of the old man, had at length started from her trance.

' 'Tis thus I would behold thee,' said his companion with emotion. ' Now thou art worthy of that great gift of Heaven—thy genius! Ah, had I possessed thy magic pencil, were I gifted with thy enchanting art, the world should have re-echoed with my name, and I might have been less unfortunate. Look at my brow. Has not sorrow written her epic there, in deep, deep lines? I lived in a world that could not comprehend me, and I was miserable. Burning thoughts, passions, genius, devoured my soul.

I could not fling them forth on canvas, nor chisel them in marble, yet my soul of fire must breathe forth or die. I flung myself in the ranks of battle against the enemies of Christendom, and honour and the laurel wreath seemed within my grasp. I was a soldier, and, before God, never have I disgraced the name. But, see here,' and he displayed a ghastly cicatrice and a mutilated trunk—'the path of life that slaked the fever of my blood has closed to me for ever. I had to resign the sword, but I could hold the pen ; and with it I drew pictures as vivid, as strongly coloured, as bold, as thy own.'

'Ay, and glorious pictures thou hast drawn, my father,' said the youth, with eager delight.

'Yet thou hast not seen my chief work,' continued the old man. 'See, here it is, on my heart ; and it shall be buried with me. It was pronounced a libel, and I was prosecuted. It has caused me many troubles, yet I love it all the more fervently.' And he drew forth from beneath his mantle a huge roll of paper, and unfolded to his eager listener that immortal tale which still enchants the world ; with its wit and mirth and madness—its fantastic Arabesques—its profound philosophy and laughter-moving folly—its episodes of tenderest love—its deep feeling and reckless humour—strange kaleido-

scope of all human passions; life itself with its
joys and sorrows, tears and smiles, phantasms
and visions, mockeries and glory, flung like a
many-coloured Iris upon the dark, dark ground
of insanity. Such was the sublime, fantastic,
all - embracing picture he enrolled before the
eyes of the young artist. The sad delirium of a
human soul, and the wild mirth that could make
even the dead to smile. And the painter forgot
his despair, his fears, his hopes, as the old man
went on, and still stood listening trancedly when
the chapter was concluded.

'Now,' said the old man, smiling with more
pleasure at the glistening emotion at the young
artist's eyes than at the homage of a multitude,
'Now, commence *thy* picture.'

'I—after what I have heard! And what
would you have me paint?'

'Paint Nature, as I have done, and thou wilt
be original, and the world shall reverence thee.
Never heed the medium tint; leave thy torn
canvas on the ground. I promise thee a better
shall arise. Only swear to me, before God, to
do as I command thee.'

'I swear,' said the youth, awed by the magic
influence of Genius.

He opened the window, prepared the palette,
stretched a new canvas on the easel, took his

colours and brushes, seated himself in silence ;
then, suddenly remembering that he had no
model, asked, inquiringly,—

'But what am I to paint?'

The old man stood leaning at the window
which looked into the street, and, without turning his head, pointed to a figure outside.

'Paint that,' he said, indicating an old water-
carrier, who at that moment was giving a
draught to some thirsty passengers.

The youth hesitated.

'Have I not told thee, copy Nature? What
matter if the object be vile and mean? Others
need a divine religion, an aureole of flame, and
angel's wings to mount to Heaven ; but Genius
reaches it by its own mighty strength alone,
without aureole or wings, or other religion than
faith in its own divinity.'

The sentiment was somewhat heterodox for
the age ; but it passed as an axiom between
the two artists, without comment or contra-
diction.

'Young man, hear me,' he continued. 'Place
those rude, dull eyes, that rude soul, on the
canvas before me, as God has placed them
there ; and thou, too, wilt be a god, and I thy
worshipper.'

In a moment the young imagination of the

artist was penetrated with the idea, and earnestly and seriously, as though Art were Religion, yet ardent as a volcano, he set himself to the task.

The old man drew forth his purse and counted out the few copper pieces yet lingering there; then, making a sign to Andreas—he who had served as model to the disgraced canvas of the preceding day—despatched him to the street. The intelligent knave at one bound pounced upon the old aguador, and in a second placed him, without a word, before the painter's easel. The youth, already plunged in the flood of rich fancies that submerged his soul, thanked his friend only with a smile. But what more was needed? At last he understood him. No word was spoken. There is something sacred in such silence. Ah, how the pencil flew along the canvas! How rapidly the varied tints were mixed on the palette and blended on the countenance in all the capricious shadows of the falling light! Thus, his beautiful head ever bent over his work, passed hour after hour of that long summer's day.

As the form grew into life, the agitation of the artist increased. Ever more intently watched that aged poet.

'Ah! he lives at last; there are the hard,

angular forms, the dull, brown tint, the matted hair, the deep, sorrow-traced furrows of that rude face! Now the bony hands start from the canvas! The poor, old, rude aguador of Seville is immortalised!'

Andreas, with beaming eyes, watched the progress of the creating hand. Once he stooped before the aguador, as if in the attitude of drinking, and the painter, without a word, transferred him to the canvas, with his *picaresque* face, vainly trying to look innocent; and so he lives in Seville yet.

The hours fled; the work proceeded.

'Good! Good!' exclaimed the ancient poet, with enthusiasm—'Thou hast done marvels.' And the young artist smiled; but suddenly a cloud passed over his brow—

'Ha! that accursed medium tint!' he exclaimed—'Can I never conquer it?' and he grasped the brush to retouch the face, when the old man seized his arm—

'Voto à Dios!' he cried 'thou shalt not. Hast thou not sworn to obey me?'

But the young man struggled hard. 'Leave me—leave me I beseech, Senhor—now, while the idea is perfect in my brain.'

'Remember thy oath.'

'What care I for oaths when my eternal fame

is at stake! Let me go,' he exclaimed frantic-
ally.

'First murder the infirm, poor old man, who
holds thy arm,' and with a force beyond his
years he barred the artist's approach to the
picture.

'Senhor! Senhor!' cried the youth, gnashing
his teeth. 'Senhor, I conjure you, let me finish
the first true work I have ever accomplished.'

'Madman, thou wouldst ruin it!'

But the painter still struggled to free himself,
and heeded him not. At length, after some
time, the old man relaxed his hold, and the
youth sprang to the easel; but astonishment
seemed to have petrified him to silence as he
stood before it. That fatal medium tint, the
rock on which he had always split, was gone.
The painting was a masterpiece.

'See, now,' said the old man, 'if I had not
reason in my words. That vapour—that misty
shadow, existed only in thine own eyes, fatigued
by long gazing on thy work—tell me, what is
wanting now to perfection? Touch it not.
Whatever it gained in softness would be lost
in genius and vigour. Contemplate thy work,
and tell me if I spoke lightly when I promised
thee eternal fame. Sign it—sign it, that thy

name may pass glorified from age to age.' And, the youth smiled gratefully on the prophet, and with a cheek bright with genius and enthusiasm, his hand trembling with the glory of success, he wrote beneath it,—

'VELASQUEZ PINXIT.'

'Diego Velasquez de Silva!' said the old man, 'thy name will be immortal!'

Velasquez threw himself, weeping with joy, upon the bosom of the old man, and exclaimed,—

'And thou, too, Miguel de Cervantes Saavedra! The words which thou hast read to me to-day will be eternal!'

'TERTIA MORS EST.'

(*A Tale from the German.*)

In the year 1665, Daniel Muller, afterwards Professor of Jurisprudence, lived at Colmar as tutor to the three sons of a certain Burgomaster of high repute in the town, named Steinberg. Now it happened that in the October of that year a travelling alchemist was received and entertained by Steinberg as his guest, and at supper, amongst other seasonable condiments, a dish of nuts being on the table, the conversation turned on their many good qualities and uses.

The three pupils of Muller were, however, entirely absorbed in their consumption, and the nuts were so rapidly seized, crushed and demolished, that Muller, as a good-natured reproof, gave them three lines to translate from the *Schola Saliterna*—

> Unica nux prodest
> Nocet altera
> Tertia mors est,

which they rendered—One nut is good, the second hurts, but the third is death.

'Well,' said Muller, laughing, 'this can hardly be true, for you have gone much beyond the third nut, yet there is no sign of death on you; so we can't believe in the *tertia mors est.*'

Scarcely were the words uttered when the alchemist started from the table in violent agitation, and, without any apology to his host, rushed from the room, leaving the company in no little amazement.

The Burgomaster at once sent his eldest son after him to know if he could in any way be of service to him, fearing he was ill. But the boy found the door of the bedroom locked to which the stranger had fled, and, looking through the key-hole, he beheld the alchemist on his knees groaning and weeping in the most violent grief, and wringing his hands, while from time to time he muttered, 'Tertia mors est! Tertia mors est!'

Shortly after the boy had returned with this strange story, a servant came in with a message from the stranger, requesting a private interview with the Burgomaster.

At once Steinberg went to the room, where he found the wretched man still grovelling on the floor in bitter despair.

'Save me,' he cried; 'save me from a shameful death. Do not betray me; do not bring me to the scaffold. You know my story and my crime. Save me! Save me! I implore you.'

The Burgomaster, much shocked at his appearance and manner, tried to soothe him, fearing that he was out of his mind; and, raising him from the ground, asked the meaning of his mysterious words.

'Do not deceive me,' said the stranger. 'You and Professor Muller must know all; that line about the three nuts proves it—*Tertia mors est.* True, oh true. The third is death—a little leaden ball. A touch of the finger and he fell. You have resolved to deliver me up to justice. I shall die the death of a felon.'

And again he flung himself on the ground with tears and groans.

Steinberg, now fully persuaded that the man was mad, still tried to soothe him, assuring him that he was perfectly safe; and even if he were guilty of any crime, they would not betray him nor give him up to justice.

At length the unhappy man grew calmer, and was persuaded to lie down, and after a little he fell into a deep sleep, as if utterly exhausted by grief and strong emotion.

But next morning, when the Burgomaster

inquired for him, they found that the stranger had disappeared, leaving no word or letter; and no tale or tidings of him after this strange scene ever came to Steinberg's knowledge. The whole mystery of his grief and despair, and the nature of his crime, if he had committed one, remained unknown.

The next year, just about the close of autumn, Steinberg and his family were again seated at the supper-table, when the dish of nuts appeared as usual with the fruit and wine, and as the sight of them recalled the strange visit and conduct of the travelling alchemist, they began to discuss his singular story with great interest and fresh expressions of curiosity.

Just then a strange lady was announced, who requested an interview with the Burgomaster; and Steinberg immediately rose to receive her and conduct her to a seat. She wore a plain but elegant travelling dress, and at once every-one was struck by her remarkable beauty and distinguished air, though her countenance bore traces of the deepest sorrow.

Steinberg felt greatly interested as he looked at her, and, placing her beside himself at the supper-table, laid a plate of nuts and a glass of wine by her side.

'No nuts, no nuts,' she exclaimed hastily,

pushing away the plate with horror, while tears
filled her eyes.

Her violent agitation, reminding them again
of the alchemist, struck the family with con-
sternation; and the Burgomaster having apolo-
gised for offering her nuts, not knowing her
dislike, politely asked in what way he could be
of service to her.

'Let me first tell you my name,' she said,
'and then you shall hear my story. I am the
widow of an eminent man, the Professor of
Chemistry at Lyons, and we lived there happily
many years; but a sad fate has compelled me
to leave my native place, and I now wish to
settle at Colmar. Here is my passport. You
will see my name inserted as the widow of
Pierre Dupont, or Petras Pontanas, late Professor of Chemistry at Lyons.'

The Burgomaster having seen that all was
correct, asked her to accompany him to his
study, where he would write introductions for
her to the leading medical men of the town.

On passing through the hall her attention
was attracted by a painting hung up on the
door leading into the study. It was a simple,
coloured sketch of a man lying on the floor of a
room, with disordered hair, and wild glaring
eyes, apparently in some crisis of strong mental

agony—but as the lady looked at it she became
deadly pale, and Steinberg, fearing she would
faint, hastily led her into the room, and placed
her in the large study chair by the table, where
she leaned her head upon her hand in the
greatest emotion.

'That picture!' she exclaimed ; 'how came it
here?   Who told you of my sad history?'
and her voice seemed choked with tears and sobs.

'We know nothing of your history, madam,'
answered Steinberg.   'That picture was done
by my eldest son, a clever young fellow, who
witnessed a remarkable scene in this very room,
and sketched it off at once with just such rude
colouring as he could find.   It represents a
stranger, an alchemist, who stopped here one
night, and was apparently suffering some deep
agony of mind.   My son saw him writhing in
mental torture on the floor, just where you are
seated—a torture that seemed like madness,
while the wild despairing cry broke from his
lips,—*Tertia mors est!* and, as you see, my son
has placed these words as a motto over the
picture.   We know nothing of the man, nor of
his story; but the painting represents him
exactly, and the terrible scene.'

'That man,' exclaimed the lady, clasping her
hands in horror, 'was my husband.   I knew the

likeness at once, and too well I know the bitter
tragedy represented by the three nuts above his
head, and the fatal words—the last I ever heard
him utter,—*Tertia mors est.*'

'Your husband!' exclaimed the Burgomaster,
'I thought you were the wife of Pierre Dupont,
the Professor at Lyons.'

'And there is his portrait,' she replied. 'Fate
has led us both to you, and I feel you have a
right to hear the whole terrible story; but I
trust to your honour that whatever I relate shall
in no way be turned to my disadvantage.

'My husband, Professor Dupont, was well off
in the world; indeed, he might have been
wealthy if his love for alchemy had not caused
him the loss of a great deal of money. I was
young, and had the misfortune of being very
beautiful; I may say so now that youth has
passed away, but then I reigned as a queen in
society. Yes, it is a misfortune to be beautiful.
I know of none greater for a woman than the
fatal beauty, that tempts men to frantic love, or
terrible despair.

'For myself, fortunately, I had a calm temperament, and I loved my husband; but all the
men that came under my influence seemed to
grow mad; and few are able to resist the eternal
solicitations and adulations that besiege a beau-

tiful woman at every moment, until, finally, dazed by the glitter of incessant homage, she yields to temptation, not indeed from love, but from weariness of the combat against the tempter, and the fatal delirium of the senses that gradually steals over her and weakens the power of resistance.

'Happily for myself, I knew little of the combat against temptation. I was neither vain nor frivolous, only fatally beautiful; and I would willingly have parted with my beauty to be at peace. I gave up my ornaments, I adopted the plainest dress, but it was of no use. Whatever I wore instantly became the rage, and was pronounced even to add to my beauty. Whether I walked or drove, or sat or stood, I was surrounded by adorers. At night I could not sleep for serenades. All day my door was besieged by letters, messages and presents ; and every week I had to dismiss some one of my servants for having accepted bribes to betray me. Two of my husband's secretaries poisoned themselves because one found out that the other was a nobleman in disguise, who had entered our service in order to be under the roof with me; and, finally, the rumour spread that I had learned the secret of making love-potions, so no man was safe who came near me,

and all the women hated me in consequence.
Thus my life was really a torture and a misery
to me, and nothing but my husband's pride in
my beauty deterred me from completely destroying it in some way or other.

'Often I asked him if my qualities of head
and heart were not sufficient to retain his love,
and if I might not destroy my fatal face by
some disfiguring preparation; but he was en-
raged at the idea. "My lovely Amalie," he
said, "if I ceased to behold your beauty, despair
would drive me mad. What supports me through
the toils of the day in the deadly atmosphere of
the laboratory, but the hope that in the evening
you will shine on me radiant and beautiful,
and make life seem paradise! You are my
heaven, my destiny; the one star in my existence; and if all the wealth I have made in my
profession went up in vapour from the crucible,
what matter, so I could still look upon your
beauty."

'In truth, he loved me passionately, though
our union was not blessed with children; this
was our only sorrow. But one evening that he
returned home unusually late, he told me that
he had met a deeply learned adept while he was
gathering herbs in the wood, and had held a
long conversation with him over occult mys-

teries; and the stranger had revealed some singular secret to him that he had learned in the East; and he even foretold the certain fulfilment of our hopes and wishes.

'That night I was startled from sleep by a movement in my room, and, sitting up, beheld the whole place lit up by a number of beautiful fine flies.

'Wondering how they had gained admission, I awoke my husband, and at the same moment perceived on the table near my bed a costly vase filled with flowers, and beside it a pile of Parisian ribbons, gloves, perfumes, dainty satin shoes, and beautiful embroidered stockings.

'Believing that they were all presents from my husband, the morrow being my birthday, I thanked him warmly; but he assured me he knew nothing of the gifts, and for the first time he seemed roused to jealousy, and with tears, and then with threats, conjured me to reveal the name of the donor, who must also certainly be my lover. I wept, but could give him no information. Then he took my keys and examined my writing-desk, but nothing was found to confirm his suspicions, and he finally left me and retired to his laboratory in a state of mad rage that filled me with terror.

'As I was dressing, the sight of my face in

the large Venetian mirror, my fatal face, with
the long golden hair falling round me like
a mantle, became hateful to me, and I was
ready to do anything desperate to mar the
beauty that was the bane of my life, when
suddenly I beheld the edge of a note half
hidden under the glass. Hastily I seized it,
and read,—

' " BELOVED AMALIA,—I am more wretched
than ever, and must fly this land ; for I have killed
a brother officer in a duel who dared to speak
lightly of you, and I am pursued by the officers
of justice. This night I stole to your room
to have one last look at your angel face, and
to leave my farewell souvenir for your birthday. Perhaps we shall meet no more, but
come, if possible, early to the little wood by
the ruined chapel. I shall wait for you under
the nut trees, and you shall hear from my own
lips all I have suffered. Be secret, but meet
me, or I shall kill myself on your threshold.

' " LUDOVICK."

' I read these words with the deepest emotion.
Cost what it would I must see him and comfort
him ; for I loved him and was about to lose
him for ever.'

' So, fair lady,' murmured the Burgomaster

'you were weak as others, and could find a place for a love next your husband in your heart.'

'Hush!' she answered with dignity. 'Do not condemn me. Wait till you hear the end of my story. When I was dressed, I packed up a few jewels for a parting gift to Ludovick, and set out with my maid, leaving word that I had gone to the bath-house, a place I often visited. On reaching it I dismissed the servant, telling her to return home and send the carriage for me in an hour.

'Then I went on alone to the wood, and there, close to the ruined chapel, I found Ludovick awaiting me.

'How can I describe the emotion, the agony of that last meeting. Our tears flowed, our kisses mingled, and then, clasped in his arms, we rested on the steps of the ruined altar, while I listened to his last sad words of love and sorrow beneath the shadow of the nut trees.

'He was fearfully excited, for he dreaded this meeting might be our last. But the parting moment approached, and I rose up resolutely to end the terrible scene, giving him, at the same time, the little packet of jewels I had selected as a souvenir. He put them back, however, exclaiming,—" No, no, Amalie, I need

no such memories. Your presence is ever with
me, and I would have shot myself last night
beside your bed, only your beauty disarmed
me. You seemed to me like a glorious angel
in your sleep, and I knelt down reverently to
utter one prayer for strength, and then I pressed
my lips upon your hand. Your good, simple
husband was sleeping calmly all the while,
quite unconscious of my presence, and then I
descended by the balcony, in the same way as
I had climbed up. Your husband knew nothing
of the midnight visitor. Poor man! science is
his true bride. I had met him in the morning
here in the wood gathering herbs, and, thinking
that I, too, was one of the sacred brotherhood,
he plunged into a deep discourse on their occult
qualities. In return I told him of a night I
passed in a convent in Armenia, when a monk
revealed to me the grand secrets, which gives
power over all things in nature. It was to
distil a living man slowly in the perfect chemical
manner, and then concentrate him slowly in a
glass. He believed all this, and pressed me to
visit him. But he little knew the manner in
which I would visit him that same night, at
the risk of breaking my neck. Oh, Amalie,
how I pity you. Childless, and wedded to this
half-mad philosopher."

'I was still a little vexed with my husband for his jealousy and harsh words, and could not help saying,—

'"Yes, truly, he does rather tire me with his long disquisitions, and I am sure he would distil me if he thought it would give him some of this mysterious occult power to which he is so devoted."

'But the hour of parting had arrived, and Ludovick pressed me to his heart in a last caress, exclaiming,—"In life or in death, my beloved, I swear to you eternal love." Then he drew down a branch of the nut tree that shadowed us, and taking three nuts, said, "Let us eat these together as a last sacrament, and when the season comes round again you will think of our last embrace beneath these branches."

'Then he broke the first nut, giving me half, and saying, as he kissed me tenderly,—"*Unica nux prodest*. No, no, that is false—it is *not* good. We are about to separate — *nocet altera*. The second hurts—true, oh true, for this is our last embrace! Oh Amalie, pray for me—forget me not. Were death even to come now it would be welcome, for I hold you in my arms, and life has no higher joy to offer. Let us then divide this last third nut for a deathless memory, even though it should bring death, and the solemn

words came from his lips as he broke it in two
—*Tertia mors est*—the last is death ! "

' At that moment a shot was fired, and Ludovick fell dead at my feet. Then a form rose up
from the shadow of the ruined chapel, and my
husband stood before me livid with rage.

' " I have heard all," he exclaimed—" *Tertia
mors est* "—and he raised the pistol in his hand
to fire at me, but I wrenched it from him, and
flung it into the bushes.

' Murderer,' I cried, ' you have killed my
brother ! Go, while there is yet time—let me
never look on your face again—here, take these
jewels, they will carry you over the frontier.
But remember, our lives are now parted for ever.
And as I thrust the packet of jewels into his
hand, a crowd of people came rushing forward ;
but my husband plunged into the wood, and I
saw him no more. Then a faintness came over
me, and I fell insensible to the ground.

' Afterwards I heard that I was carried to the
carriage and brought home, while my poor
brother's dead body was laid in the court-house
to await the official examination.

' I was the only one capable of giving information as to his death ; but, fortunately, as I may
say, a brain fever laid me me up for weeks
after, and the doctors having declared that all

allusion to the past might be fatal to me, the inquiry was allowed to rest, and there was no public trial.

' But evil tongues did not rest.   All the women who envied my beauty poured their venom on me, and all the men whose advances I had repelled mocked and derided my claims to superior virtue.   The rumour, also, that the murdered man was my brother, heightened the scandalous imputations.   Everyone strove to tread me in the dust and triumph over my vaunted beauty, while they flung their scorn on my tragic fate, so that life, at last, became insupportable, and I would have made an end of the horrible torture, only, just then, a letter came from my husband.   He was safe for the present, he said, and already on his way to Denmark, where he meant to live and practise his profession under another name, and the country he left should hear no more of him.   But before his departure he had drawn up a document making over to me all his property, and this deed, properly signed and witnessed, would be forwarded without delay.

So, then, I was free.   The deed arrived in due course, and I immediately took steps for the sale of our house and property ; and having realised a large sum for investment in the bank,

I felt secure as to the future, and able to arrange my life as seemed best to me, without let or hindrance.

'But I hated the world and society, and my first move was to enter a convent as a lay sister, and devote myself to works of charity and attendance on the sick. My services were highly valued, for I had acquired a great knowledge of medicine from my husband's teaching; and so my life passed smoothly on for some years, till evil tongues ceased to revile me, and I was left in peace.'

'Your misfortunes touch me deeply,' said the Burgomaster. 'Yet I confess that your brother's words might well excite suspicion, and your husband may be pardoned for the fatal result of his very natural jealousy. But was your brother indeed your lover? And how could you permit so dreadful an entanglement?'

'Ah, sir,' she replied, 'his love was a misery to me, and I did all I could to turn his mind from the passion, which became almost a madness, for my fatal beauty seemed to have turned his brain; so at last he resolved to leave the country and see me no more. That very night he meant to quit me for ever. But the passion and the madness are now extinguished with his life. My husband had never seen him, but his

Y

suspicions were aroused by the presents; and, hearing that I had gone to the bath-house, he followed, bringing his pistols. There the women told him that I had left for a walk in the wood; then he remembered the stranger he had seen there gathering flowers and glow-worms, and suspicion became certainty. He followed me to the ruined chapel, and, hiding in the shadow of the wall, watched us. and listened to our conversation. At the last words—*Tertia mors est*—he fired, and the deed of death was done.'

'Ah, wretched man!' exclaimed the Burgomaster. 'Can you not pardon him? Will you not see him again and give him your forgiveness?'

'No human eye will see him more,' she answered. 'He has passed before the judgment-seat of God. But I forgive him; yet he could not forgive himself. For eight years he lived at Copenhagen under an assumed name; and his learning and skill soon gave him wealth and position, and he became State Alchemist to the King of Denmark, who was passionately devoted to the Secret Science.

'Still, however, the memory of the murder haunted him, and he became strange and unsettled in his mind. The sight of nuts always affected him, and brought on a crisis of grief and tears. So at last he resolved to travel, in hopes of gaining peace of mind. It was then you saw him; and after that scene in your house he went back to our old home, and was seen, at the ruined chapel in the wood, prostrate under the shadow of the nut trees. But no one recognised him. He seemed only a feeble, white-haired old man, and they thought him crazed. Then, after some days, he disappeared. But his soul was filled with a strong purpose; the hour of retribution had come, and he deliberately gave himself up to justice, and confessed his crime.

'While in prison he wrote for me to come to him, and there in the prison-cell was our last meeting. We prayed and wept together, and then he told me all, and of his meeting with you; and he charged me to go to you after his death and narrate the whole dreadful story, and bring you his deep gratitude for your words of kindness and sympathy.

'The next day, in presence of an immense concourse of people, he was conveyed to the scaffold, which was erected just beside the ruined chapel in the wood, where the murder had been committed.

'There he knelt down and prayed, while I knelt beside him and held his hand. Then he plucked three nuts from the tree waving above us—the very tree where Ludovick had gathered his death-fruit — and, dividing them with me, as had done, pronounced the fatal, well-remembered words, embracing me in a last farewell, for the terrible moment had arrived. They carried me half fainting to the chapel, where I sank prostrate on the steps of the ruined altar but his voice still rang clear in my brain,—

Unica nux prodest,
Nocet altera,
Tertia mors est.

And then the heavy fall of the sword of the executioner followed the words, and I knew that his miserable existence had ended on earth.'

The Burgomaster was deeply touched at the lady's story, and, taking her hand, promised to be her faithful friend for life, and, if possible, to alleviate her affliction by his care and sympathy; but as his tears fell upon the hand that he held in his own, he observed a ring on her finger that riveted his gaze. That ring, she said, was my poor brother's. It had belonged to our dear father, and I always wear it for the sake of its sacred memories ; see, here are my father's initials, P. R.

'And the name?' asked the Burgomaster eagerly. 'The name of your father; of your family?'

'My father's name was *Paul Rochet*,' answered the lady; 'and he resided at Montpellier. Have you heard of him? He was well known as a leading physician.'

The Burgomaster seemed unable to speak from agitation, but, going to his desk, drew out some papers carefully arranged and tied.

'Tell me,' he said, and his hand trembled with excitement as he unfolded the papers; 'tell me the age of your brother; if he were living now.'

'Forty-six years old this very day,' she replied.

'Right, all right!' exclaimed the Burgomaster, with joyful eagerness. 'He is forty-six years old to-day, and he is living, Amalie. There is a strange mystery to unfold, but I have the proofs here. If the unhappy Ludovick loved you, there was, at least, no sin. He was not your brother. It is I who claim you for a sister; listen to the strange story. Your mother's nurse changed two infants that were in her care, both being of the same age; and it was her own child, the son of Maggi the artisan, who was reared in your father's house as his heir, while I, the true heir, was brought up by Maggi, and lived with him till his death, know-

ing nothing of my parentage. But I had
intellect and ambition, and after Maggi's death
I removed here, far away from all early associations, and took the name of Steinberg, that
nothing might be known of my obscure artisan
life, and here I have attained wealth and honour
and a high official position. Amalie, you need
not fear to receive me as your brother, nor as
your father's son, nor for the proofs of my
strange tale.

'Some years ago I was summoned to take the
deposition of a dying woman in one of our
hospitals; but when I arrived she was almost
at the last gasp and unable to utter a word.
She had only strength enough to me hand a
packet, on which was written 'The Confession
of Liza Maggi,' and then she fell back dead.

'Here is the document. In it she tells the
story of how she changed the children, that
her son might be reared in affluence as the heir,
but, unfortunately, she only gives the initals
of your father's name, P. R., and no clue whatever
to his place of residence.

'However, strangely enough, she mentions the
beautiful Amalie, who was brought up with
Ludovick as his sister, and she expresses bitter
sorrow for her sin, for she now knows that
her son adored the lovely Amalie, and. if the

truth were known, there might be no hindrance
to the marriage. Therefore, feeling that death
was on her, she wrote her confession, and promised full evidence of all before a magistrate.
But, as I said, she died before the word was
uttered that could have revealed to me the
history of my parentage.

'It was only when I saw the initials on your
ring, and thought of your sweet name, Amalie,
that the truth flashed on me, and I felt that
you were indeed my own, long lost beautiful
sister. Oh, Amalie, will you not receive me
now with trust and affection, and let me con-
secrate my life to your happiness.'

Her only answer was a flood of tears as she
flung herself with emotion into his arms.

'Amalie,' he said, tenderly caressing her,
'let us thank God, who has brought light out
of the darkness. While to me he has given
a name, a heritage, and a loved and lovely
sister.'

'Stay with me, Amalie, and let our lives be
united in the bonds of sweet relationship.'

'No, my dear brother,' she answered sadly.
The dead stand between me and the living. I
shall go back to my work in the holy sisterhood
of mercy, and find rest and peace at last beneath
the shadow of the cross. But your spirit will

be with me, for through you the doom has been lifted from our family, and the tragic drama has ended which began and closed with the fatal words that will never leave my memory—*Tertia mors est*—the third is Death.

THE END.

COLSTON AND COMPANY, PRINTERS, EDINBURGH.

Lightning Source UK Ltd.
Milton Keynes UK
175696UK00001B/22/P